18 Italian Songs for Accordion Duet

Carole Gatwood

The Am-1100 concert accordion on the cover is courtesy of Petosa Accordions.
The Colombo Pro 96 accordion on the cover is courtesy of Accordions International.

WWW.MELBAY.COM

Foreword

Accordionists, you are going to be amazed with this new book of eighteen Italian songs. They are written in a very interesting, engaging, and superbly professional style. The parts have musical ornaments, fills, bass solos and very complementary harmony. These duets have ranges of close to two octaves on the accordion. You can close your eyes and imagine you are hearing a group of musicians performing these arrangements. The arranger of this book is Carole Gatwood. She is a very talented music arranger for cello and is now venturing into the world of accordion duets. She and her husband Craig Rifel, both retired career Detroit Symphony musicians, are now studying and performing as an accordion duo.

Each duet in this book has been arranged to enhance the melody line with ornaments, a variety of fills and reed registrations to blend the melody and accompaniments together. The Italian flair of the music is obvious to the listener. I would have enjoyed playing duets so well-voiced as these in the many accordion competitions and Italian festivals I played in over the years with my duet partner. Here now is a book with wonderful duet arrangements for accordionists of all ages and ability. These will be wonderful additions to their repertoire.

Whether you play acoustic or digital accordion, this book of Italian songs will inspire you to play duets, trios, quartets and perhaps even join an accordion club wherever you live. Playing music together helps you develop your musicianship skills, timing, musical ear, and dynamic expression, with the added benefit of having fun creating music together. This is why I have been a professional accordionist, career music teacher and have played in bands my entire life. The experience is incomparable. I know that in this book you will soon find your favorite duet.

All the best.
Gordon Kohl
Professional Accordionist and Teacher.

Introduction

These charming folk songs of the 1800s, many of which are little-known outside Italy, have been a delight to make into duets. I created the arrangements to play with my husband. With Gordon Kohl's encouragement and vision, what started with one song, "Cielo, Come Mi Lasci!", has expanded into this book of 18 duets. These arrangements are designed to be accessible to the intermediate accordionist. The duets have equally involved right hand parts, and because they share the melody, neither is clearly the 'primo' part. Therefore, I named the part with both hands "Accordion II" and the other "Accordion I". In passages where the parts are in sixths or a descant line is higher than the tune, I have written "melody" to identify the prominent voice.

About the music:

-Where there is a fingering such as 4 – 5, this means one should substitute the 5th finger for the 4th while holding the key down. This is a traditional organ fingering method.
-Look for footnotes in various songs that can help with bass & chord usage.
-The left-hand is in Master.

The spirited "Trippole Trappole" is our opener whenever my husband and I perform so it appears first in the book. To get acquainted with the collection, I suggest first looking at "A Me Mancano i Termini" or "Nici, Ricordati".

I wish you many good times with the Italian songs in this book!

Carole

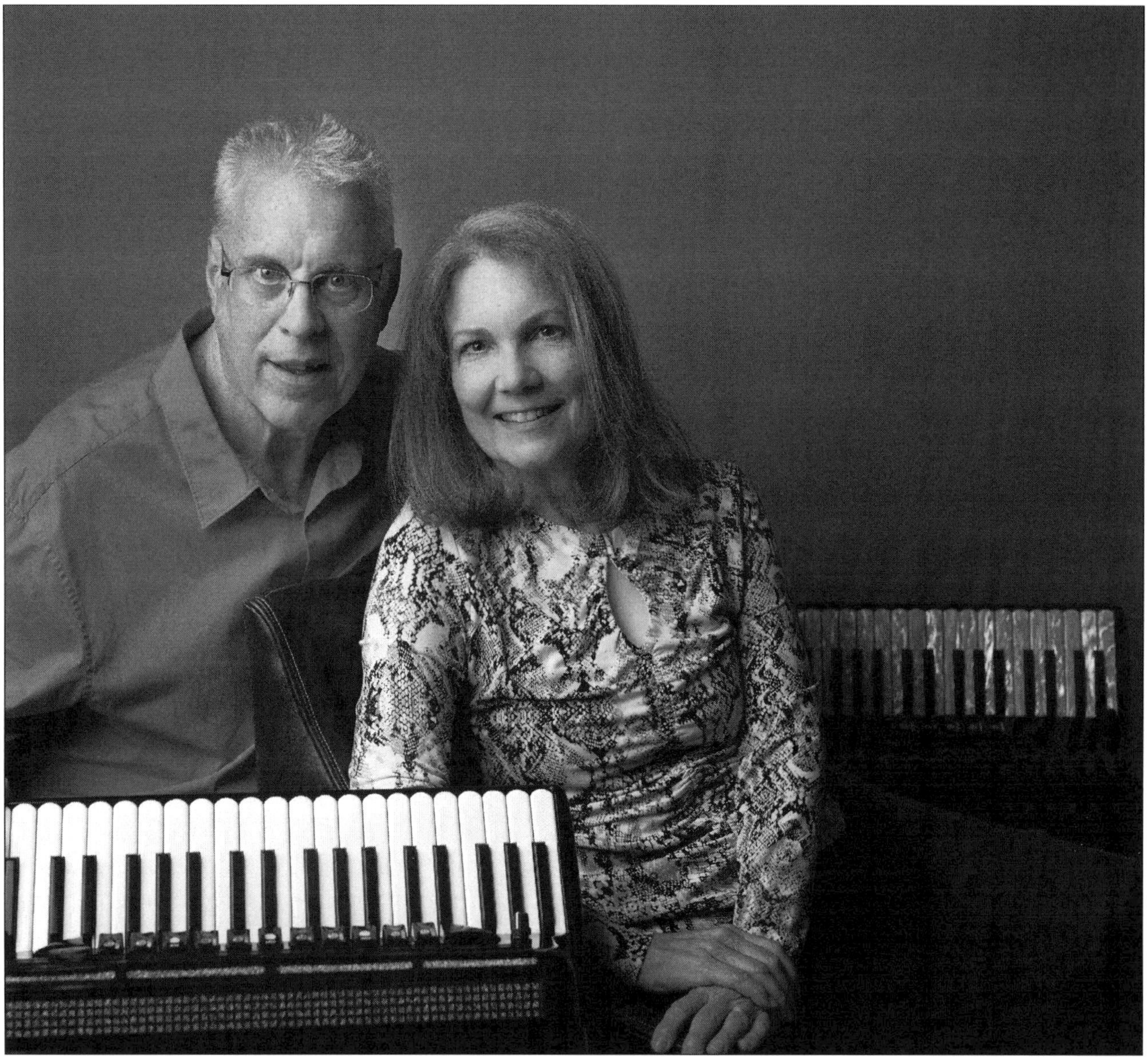

Photo by Studio 120 Photography

The author, Carole Gatwood, with duet partner and husband, Craig Rifel.

Carole Gatwood received a Bachelor's and a Master's Degree in Cello Performance from Indiana University School of Music. She was a member of the Detroit Symphony Orchestra cello section for 31 years. While also raising a family, one of her creative activities was arranging music for cello and cello ensemble. In retirement, after moving to San Diego County, both Carole and her husband, Craig Rifel, began serious study of the accordion with teacher Gordon Kohl. They perform duets in their community.

Contents

Trippole Trappole

Popular Neopolitan Song of Spanish Origin

Guglielmo Cottrau
Arr. by Carole Gatwood

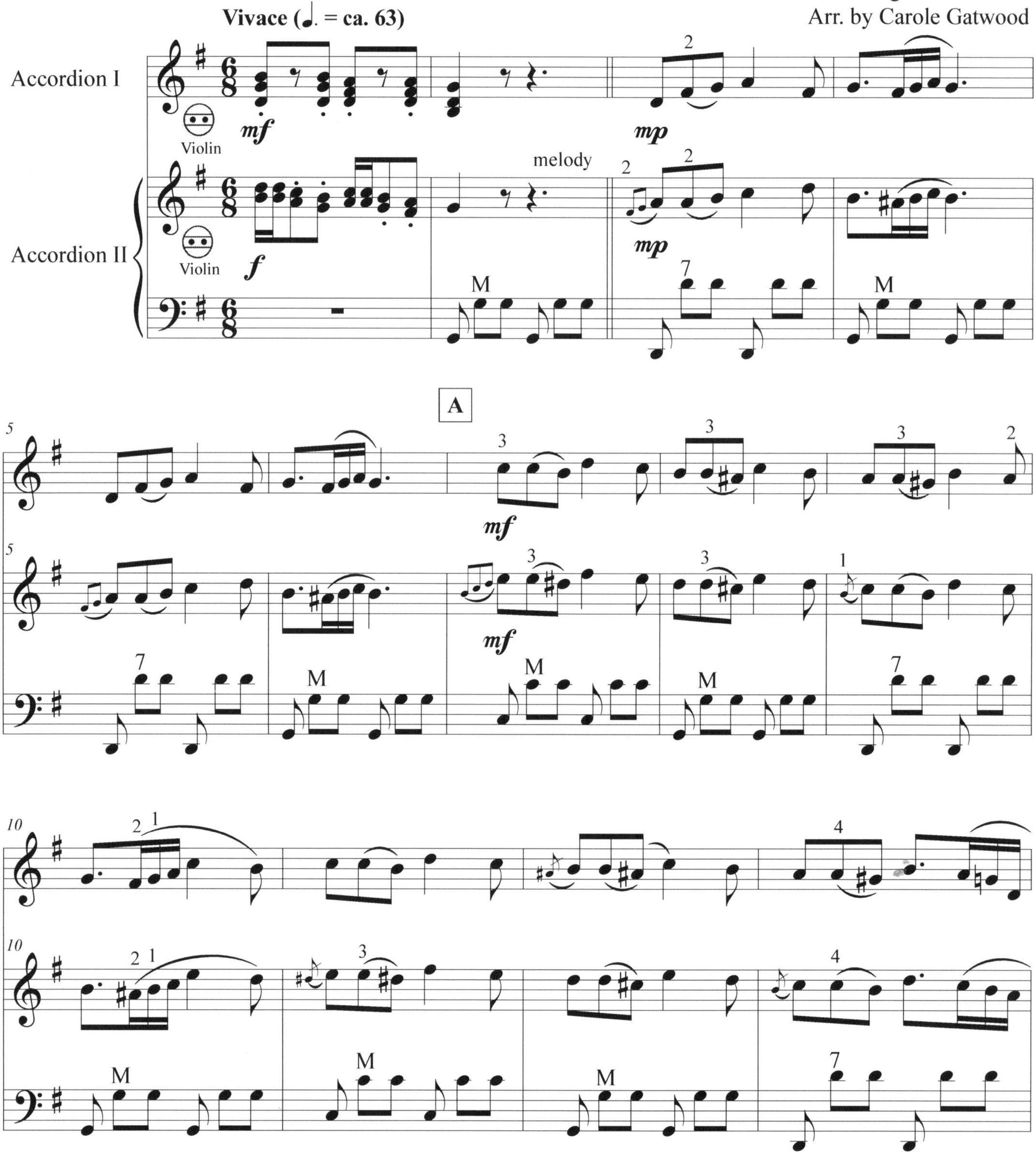

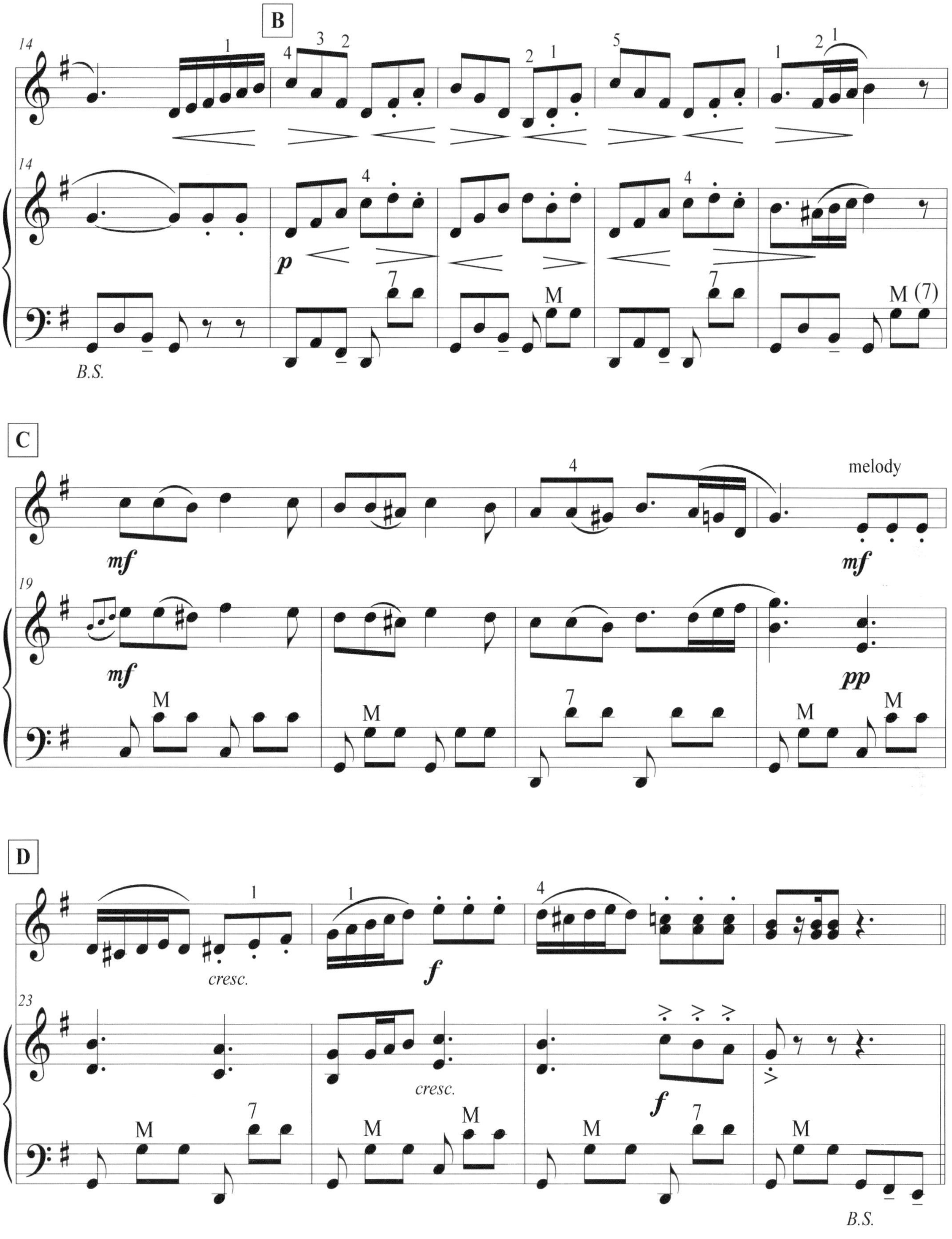
B
14
I
II
p
7
M
M (7)
B.S.
C
19
mf
melody
pp
D
23
cresc.
f
B.S.

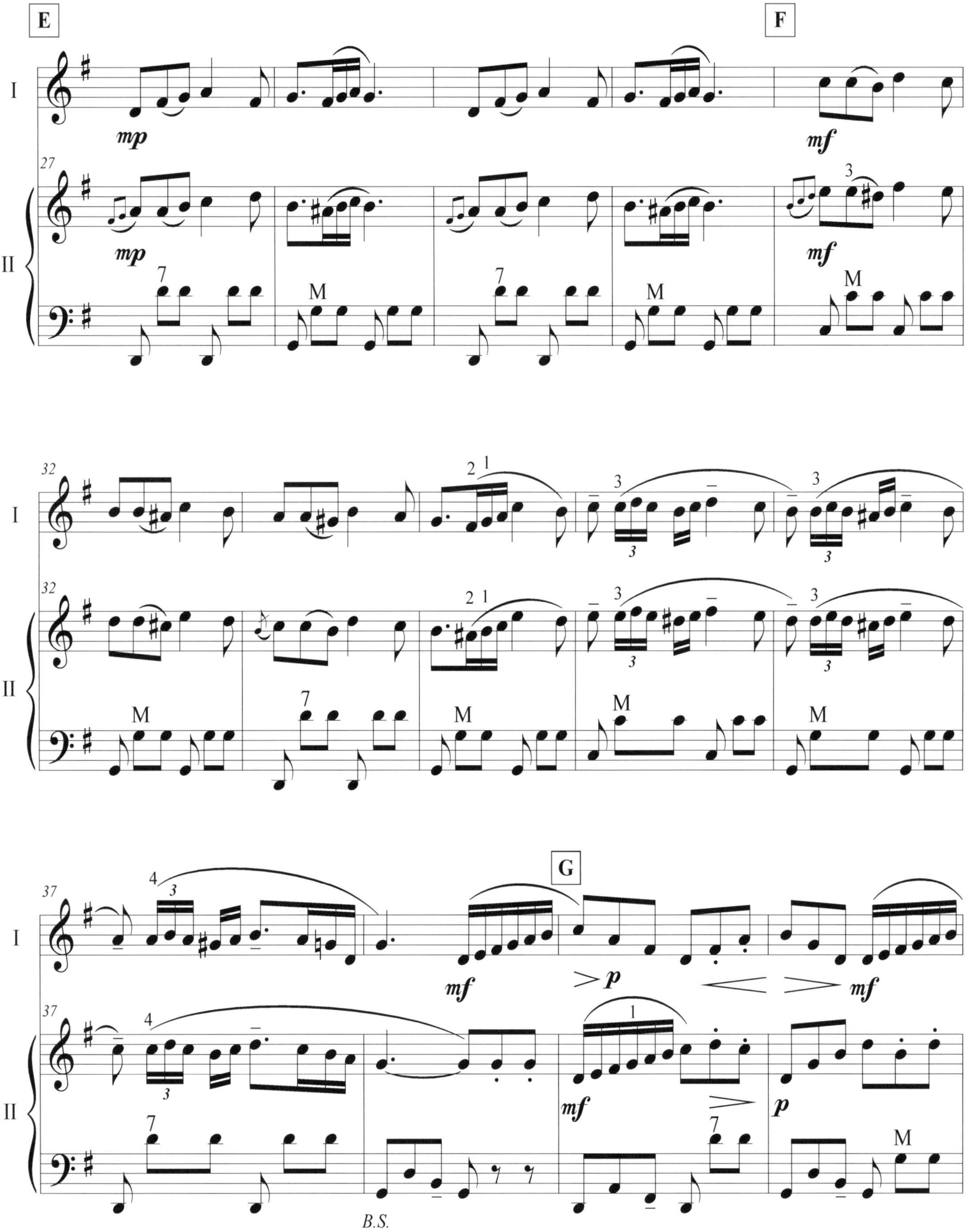
E
F
G
I
II
27
32
37
mp
mf
p
M
7
B.S.

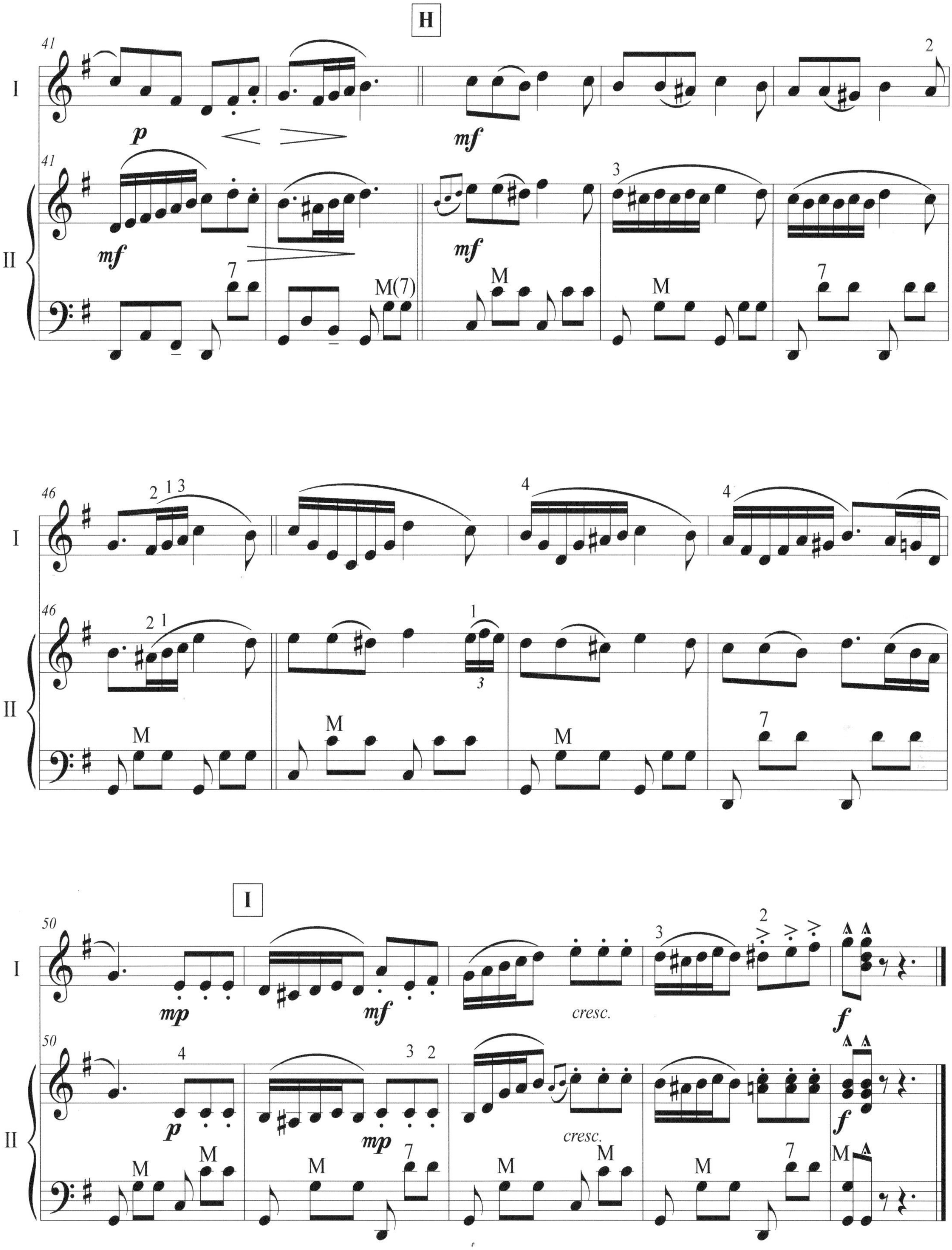
H
I
II
p
mf
M(7)
M
cresc.
f

A Me Mancano i Termini

"I don't have the words to tell you (of my devotion)"

Sicilian
Arr. by Carole Gatwood

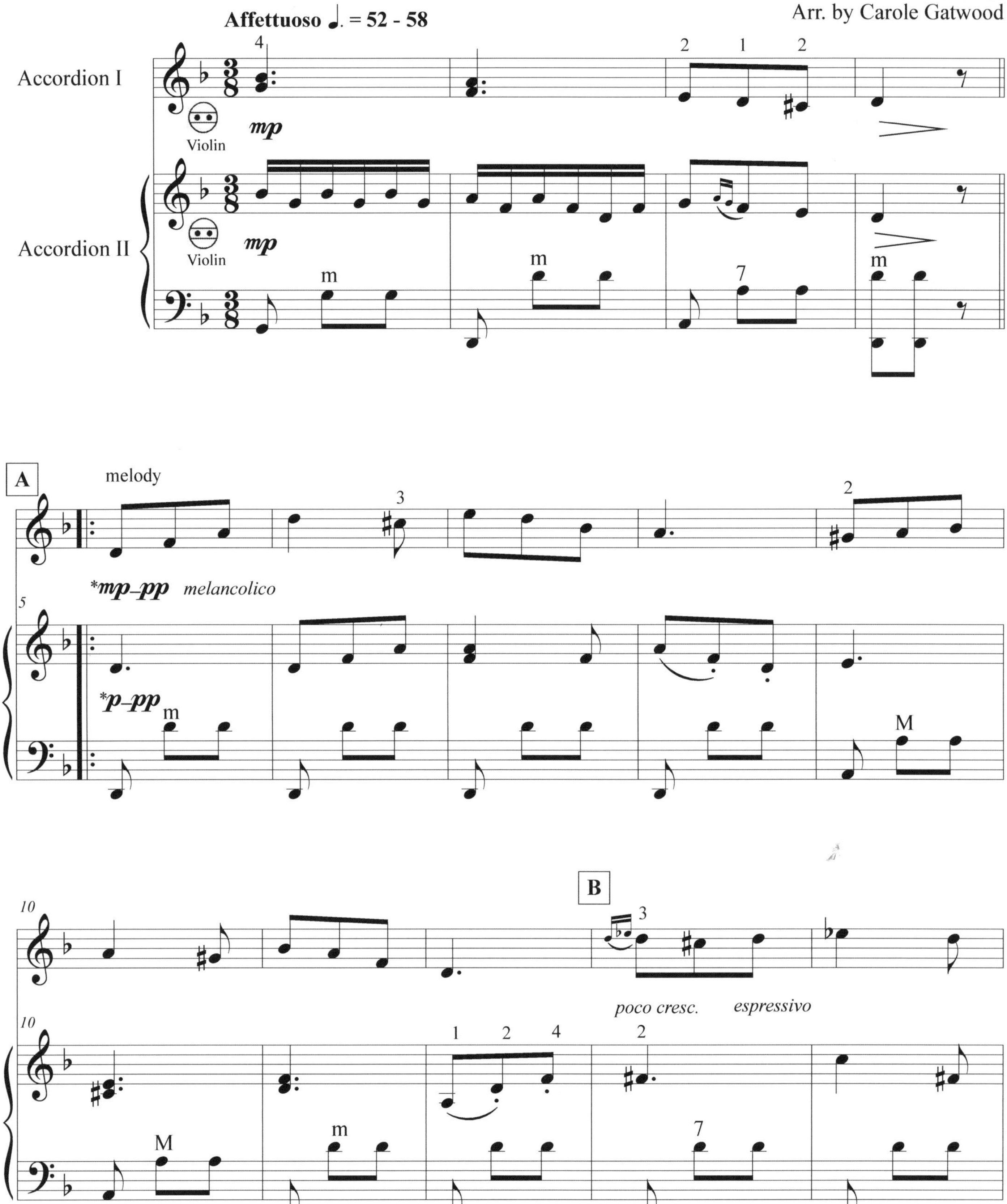

*Please observe the first dynamic the first time through and the second dynamic on the repeat.

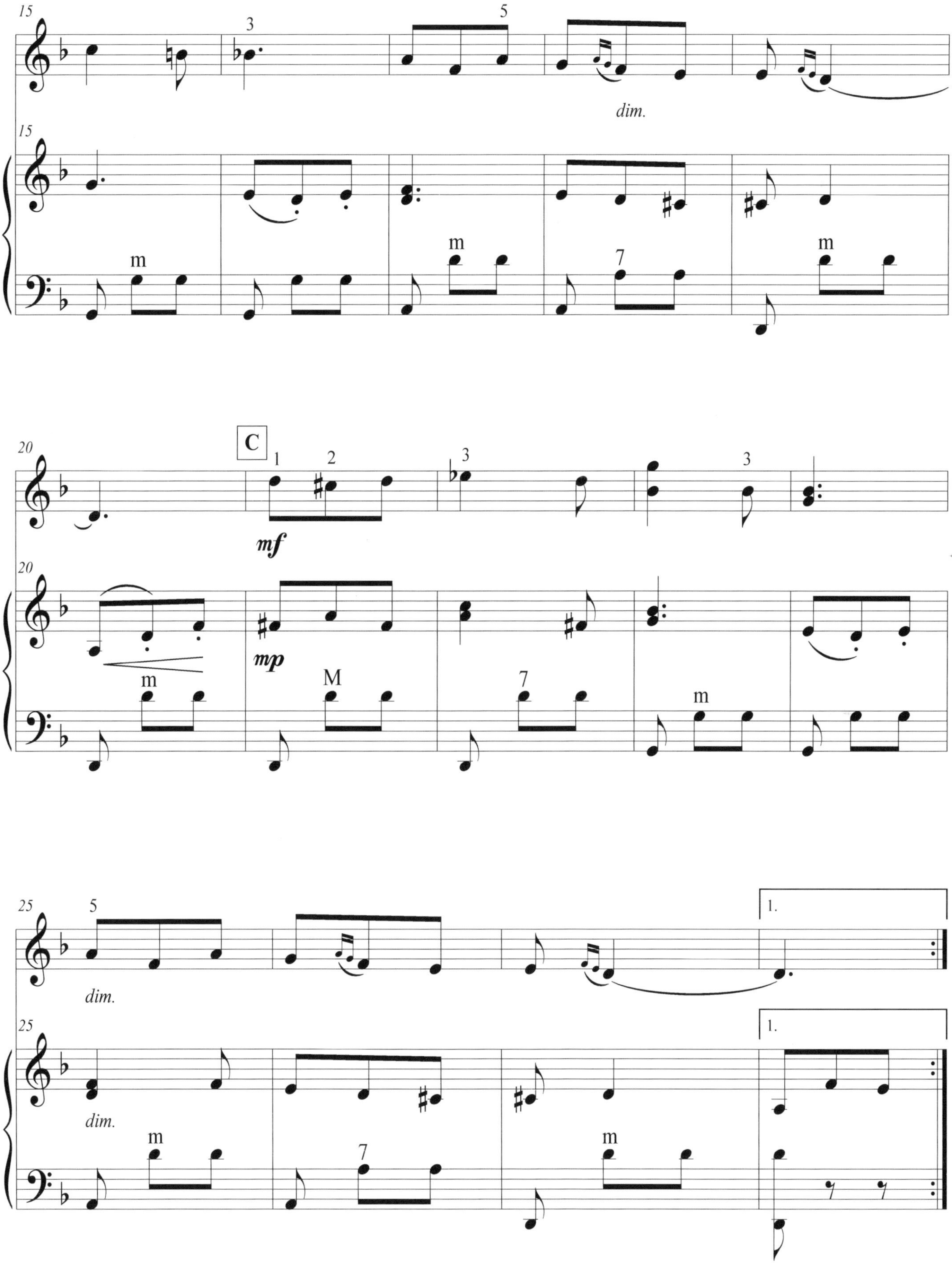
I
II
dim.
C
mf
mp
m
M
7
1.

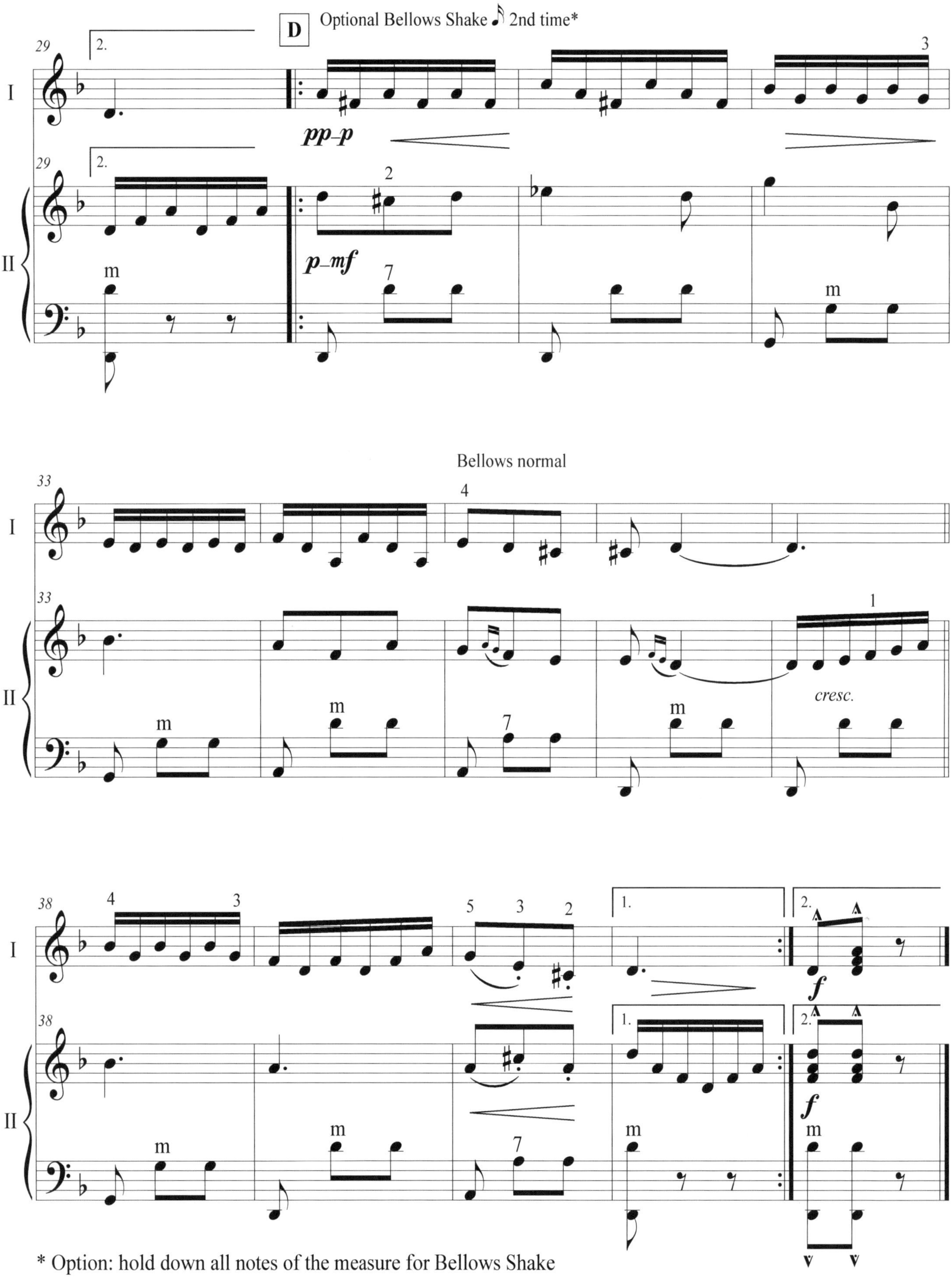

* Option: hold down all notes of the measure for Bellows Shake

Il Granatello

Neopolitan Folk Song
Arr. by Carole Gatwood

Lento (♪ = ca. 120)

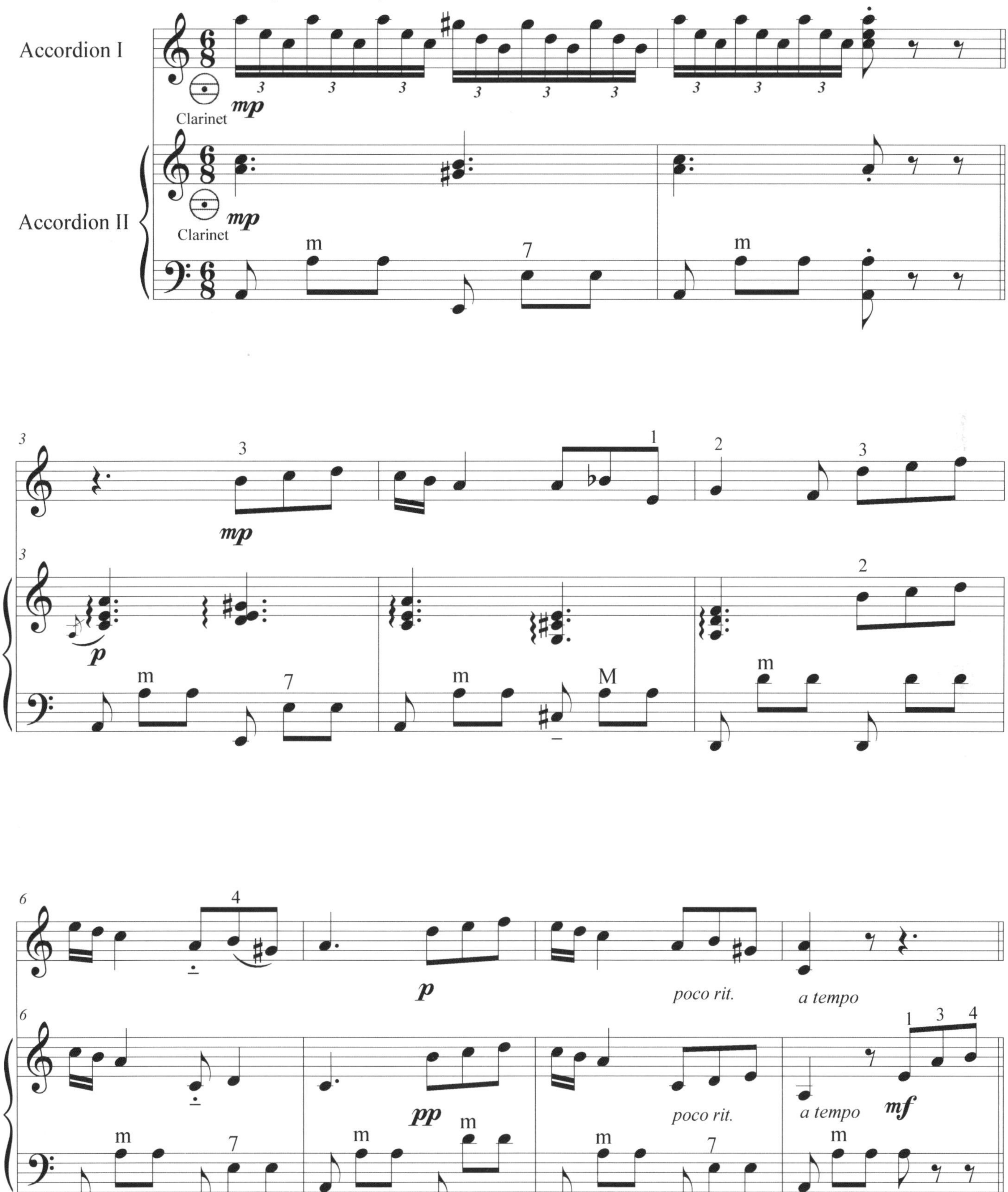

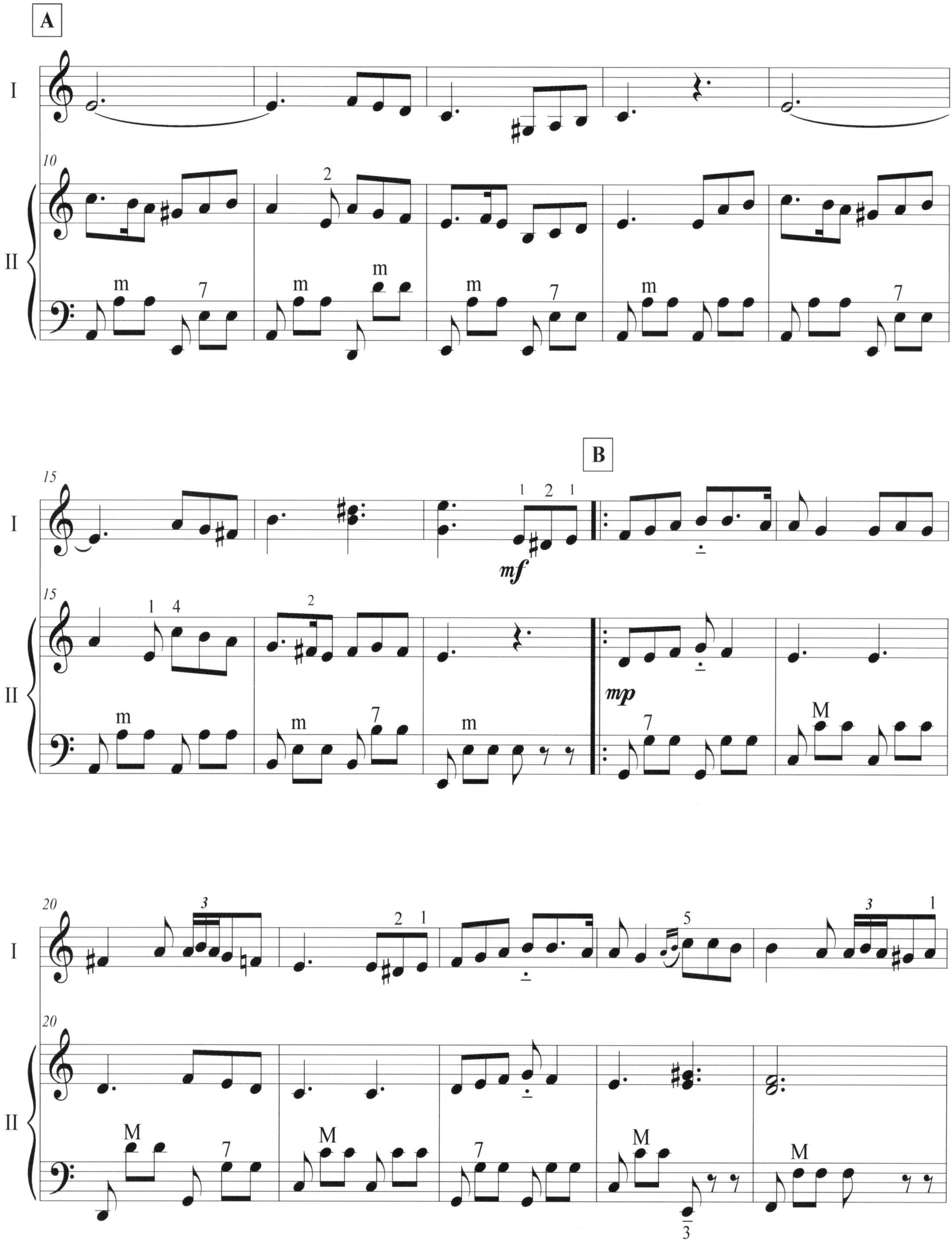
A
I
II
m
7
M
B
mf
mp

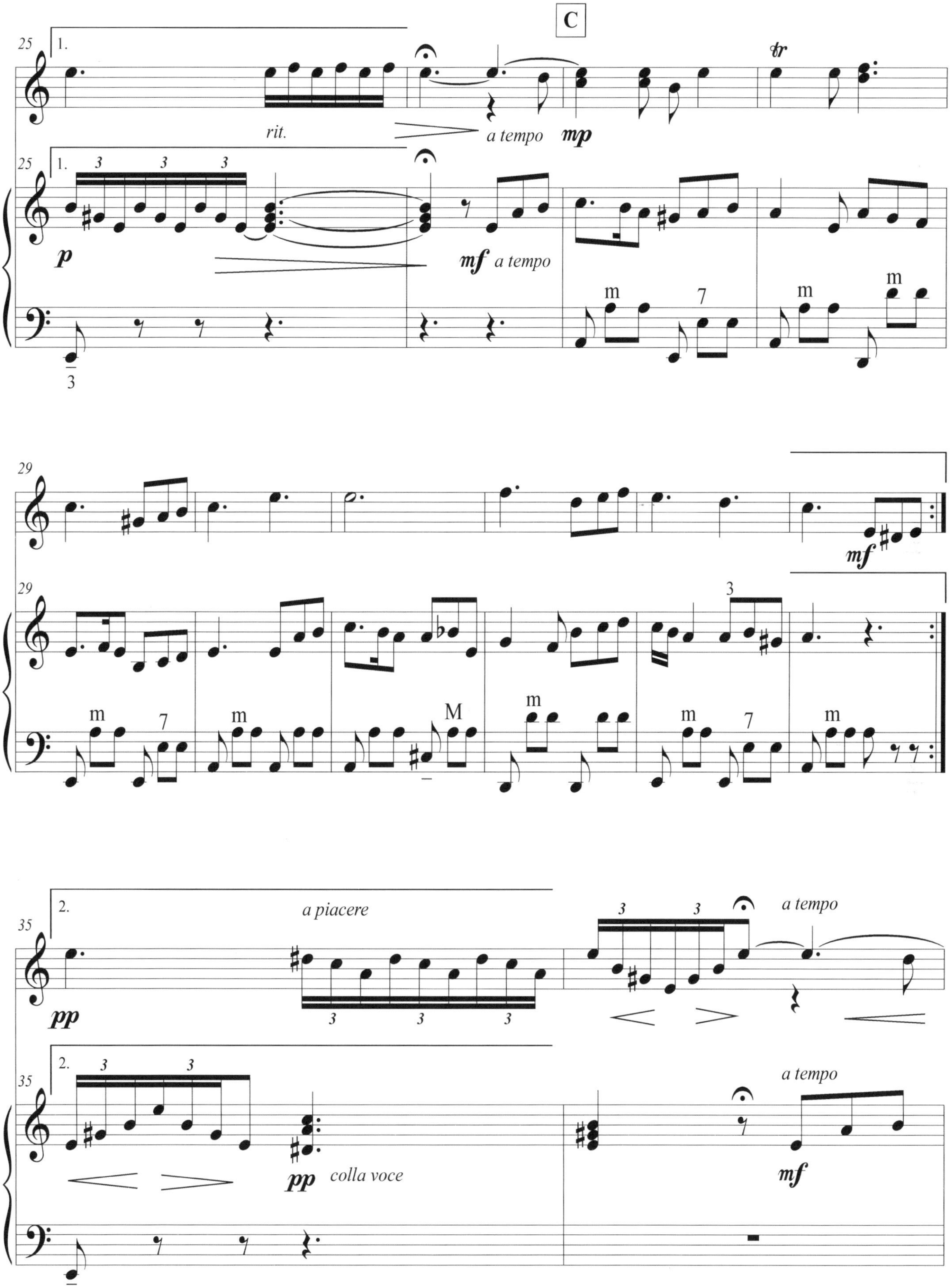
C
1.
rit.
a tempo
mp
mf a tempo
tr
2.
a piacere
pp
colla voce
a tempo
mf

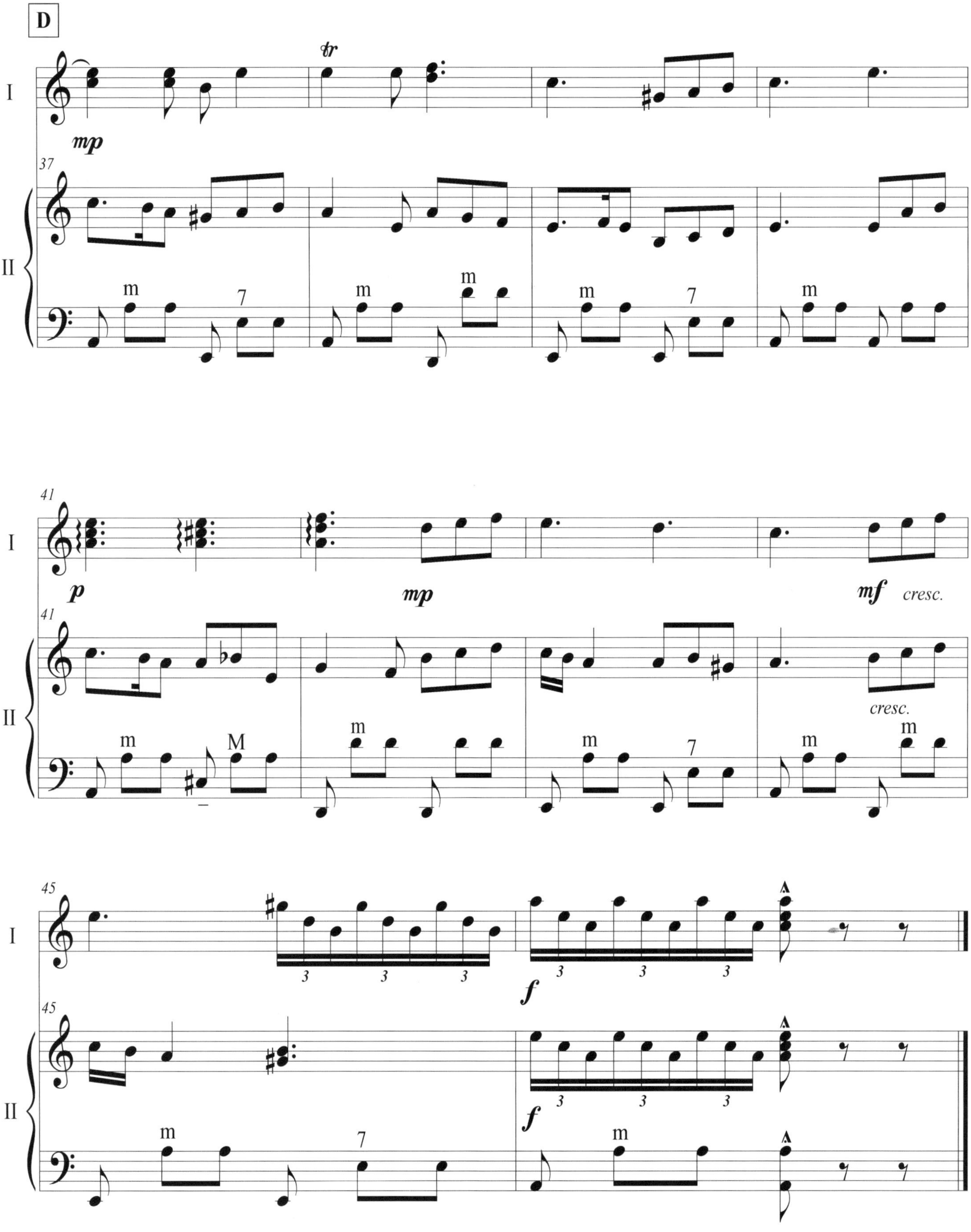
D
I
II
mp
tr
37
m
7
41
p
mp
mf
cresc.
M
45
3
f

Cielo, Come Mi Lasci!

"Heaven, how you have left me suffering!"

Sicilian
Arr. by Carole Gatwood

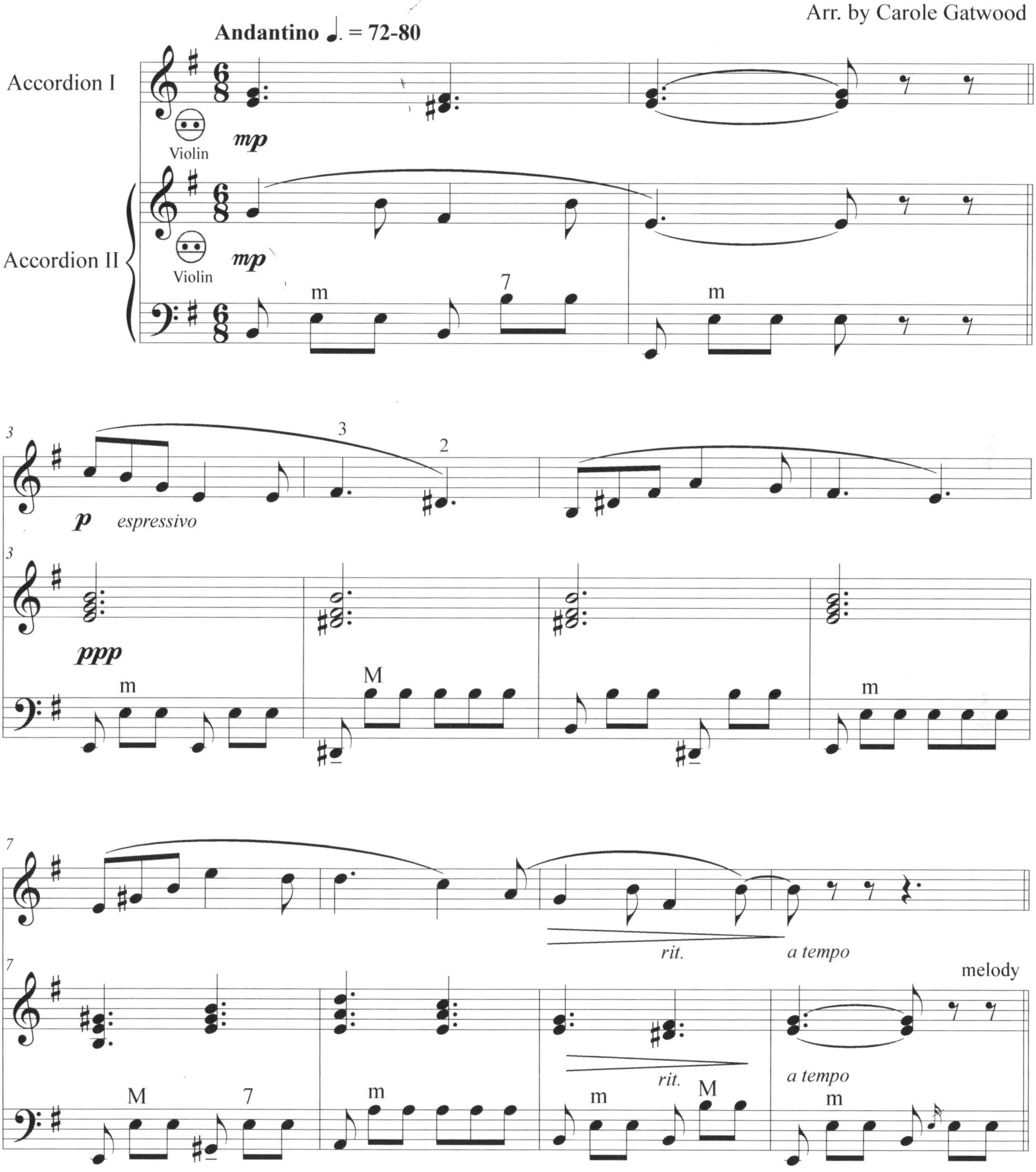

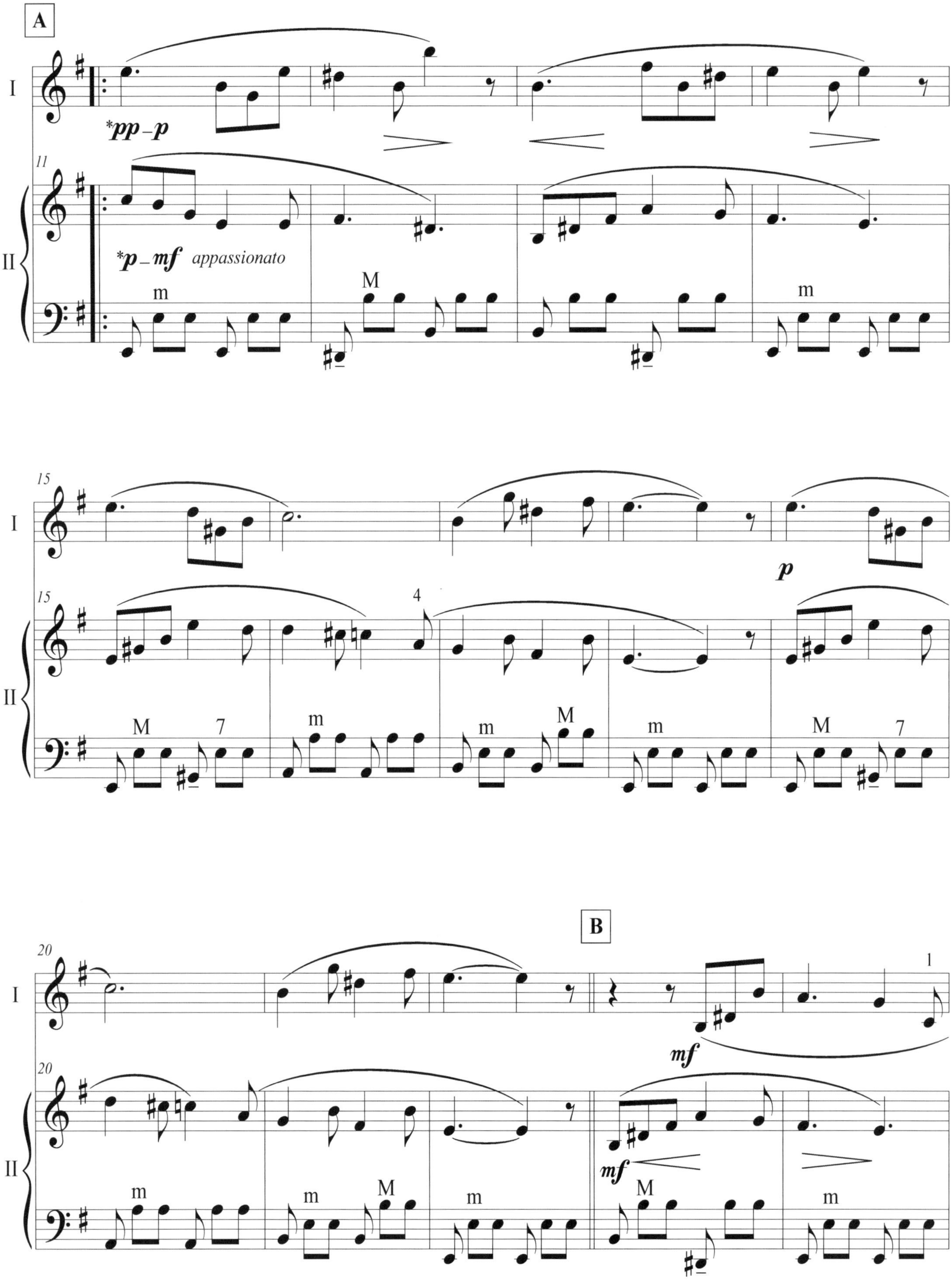

* Please observe the first dynamic the first time through and the second dynamic on the repeat.

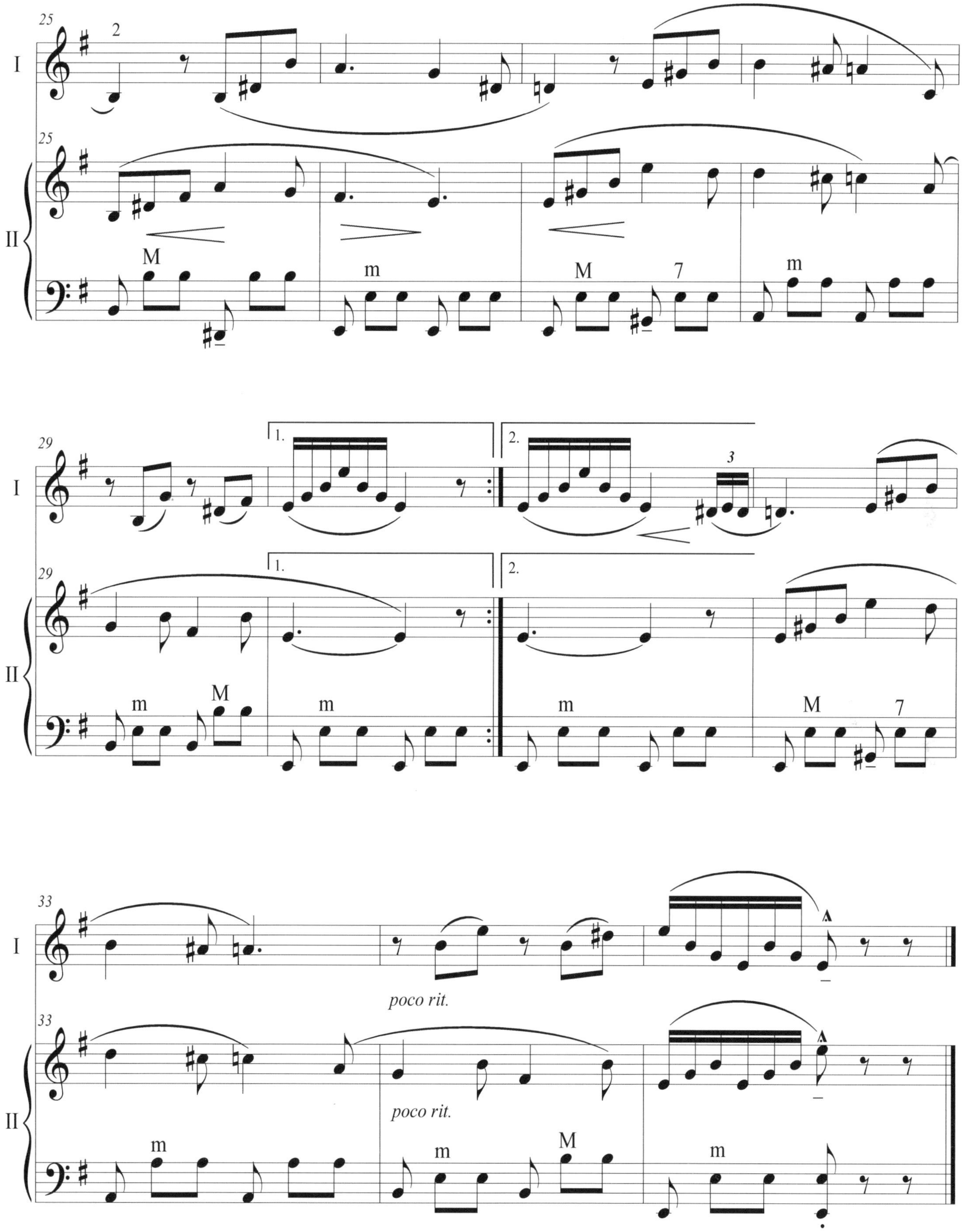
25
I
II
M
m
7
29
1.
2.
3
33
poco rit.

La Carolina

Canzone Napolitana di Castellamare

Arr. by Carole Gatwood

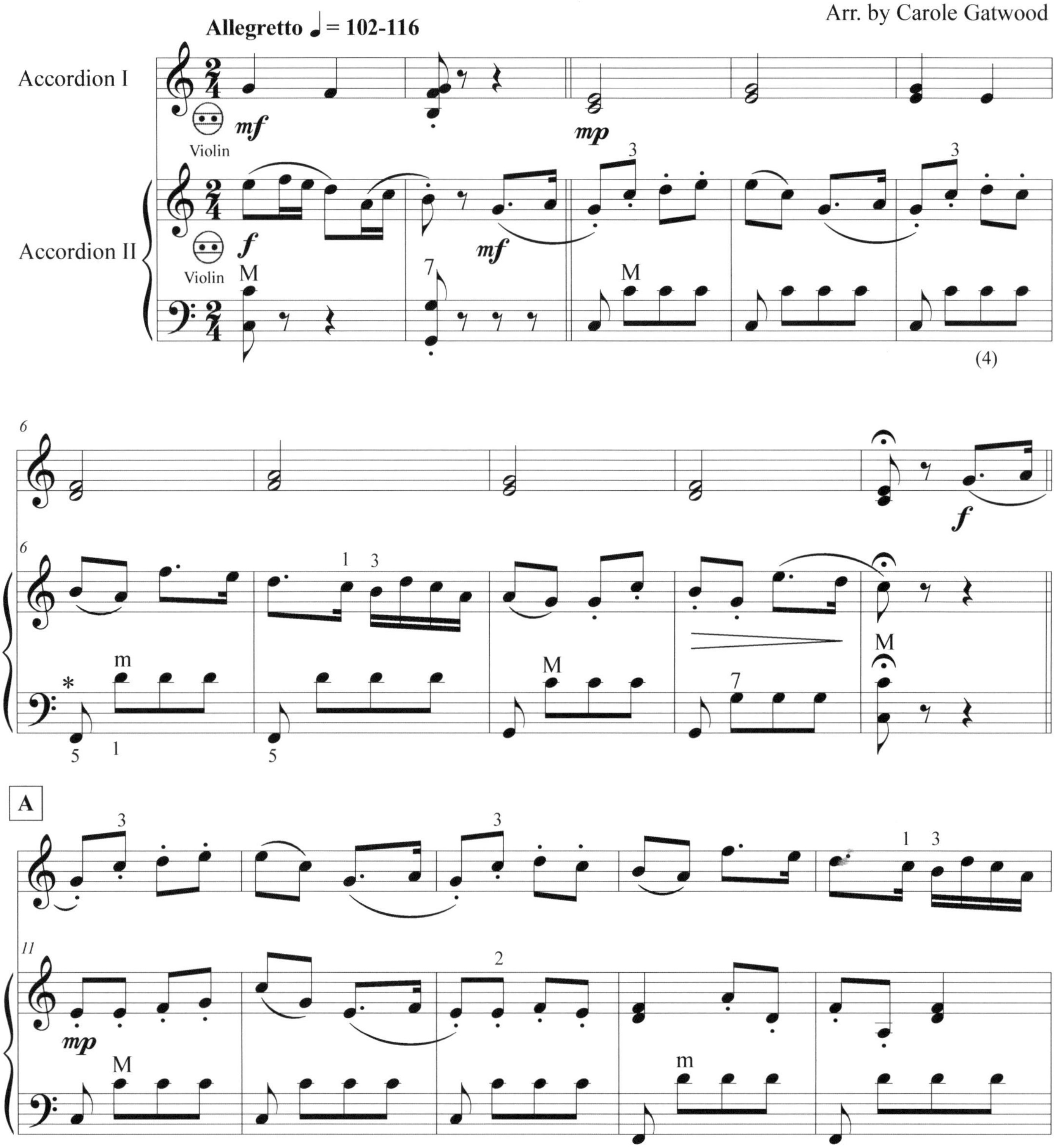

*Optional: In measure 6 & 7 a D Bass & minor chord may be played.
The same configuration occurs two more times in this folk song.

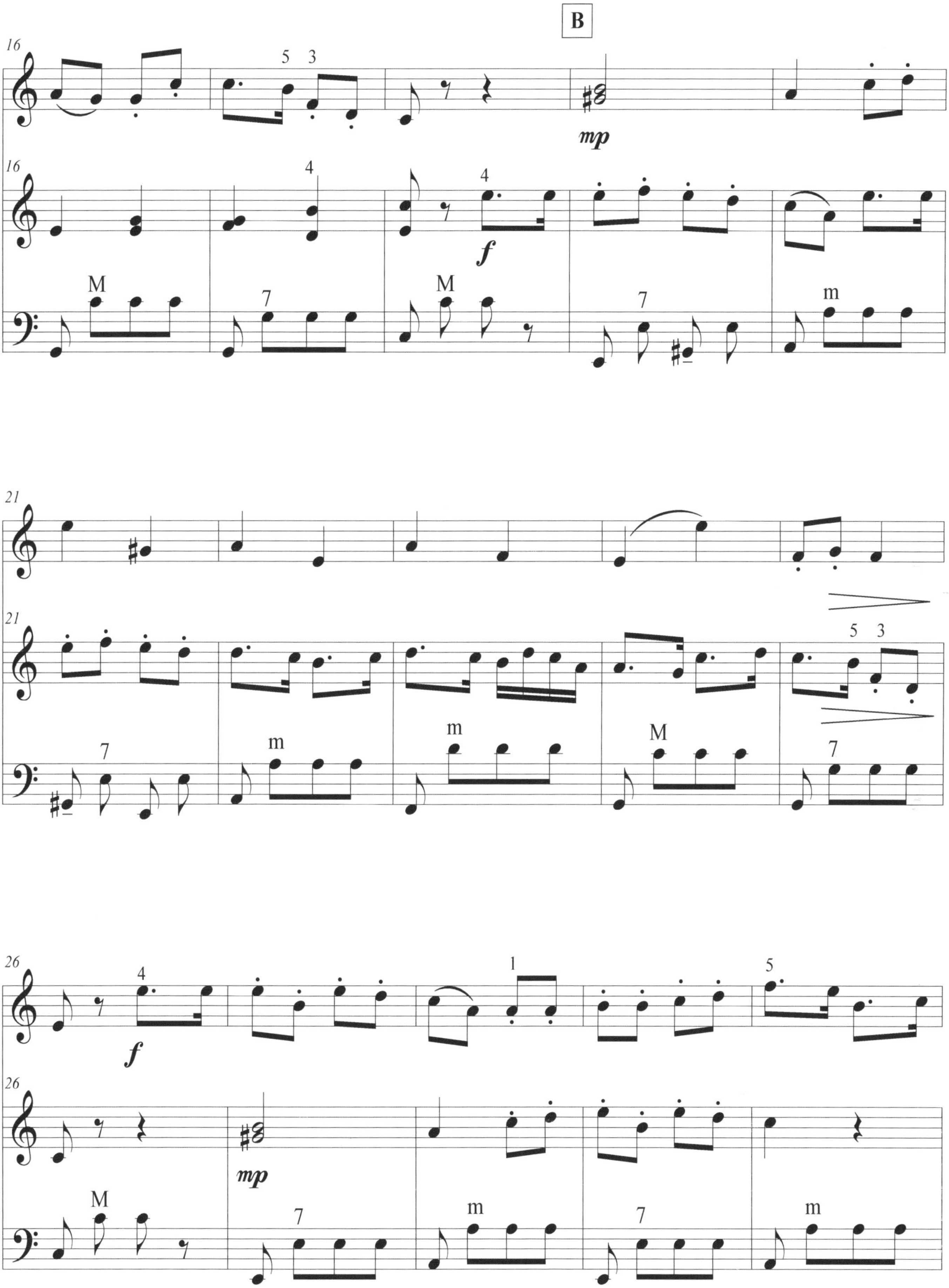
B
I
II
mp
f
M
m
7

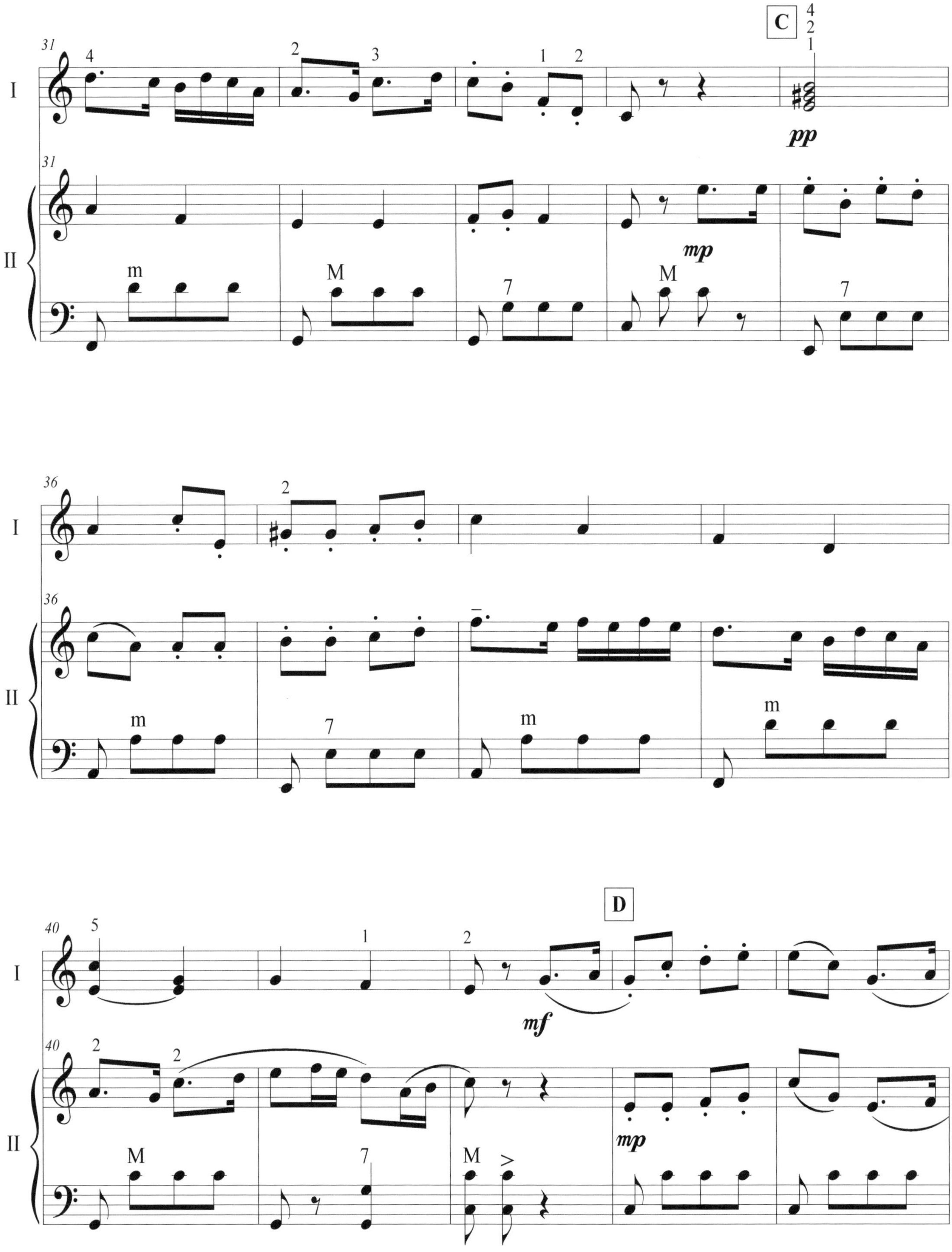
C
D
I
II
pp
mp
mf

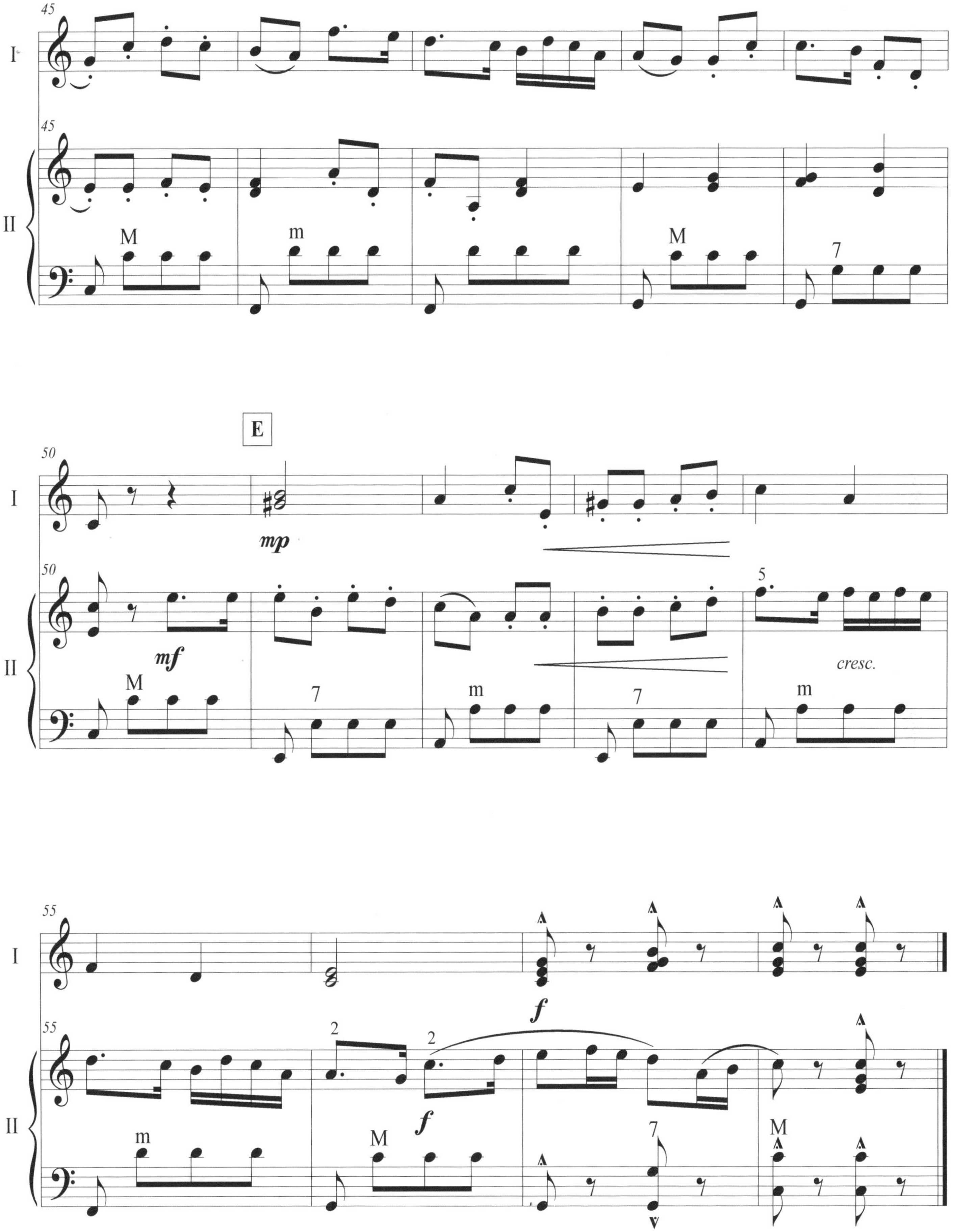
I
II
M
m
7
E
mp
mf
cresc.
5
2
f

Nici, Ricordati

A Sicilian song of reminiscing

Arr. by Carole Gatwood

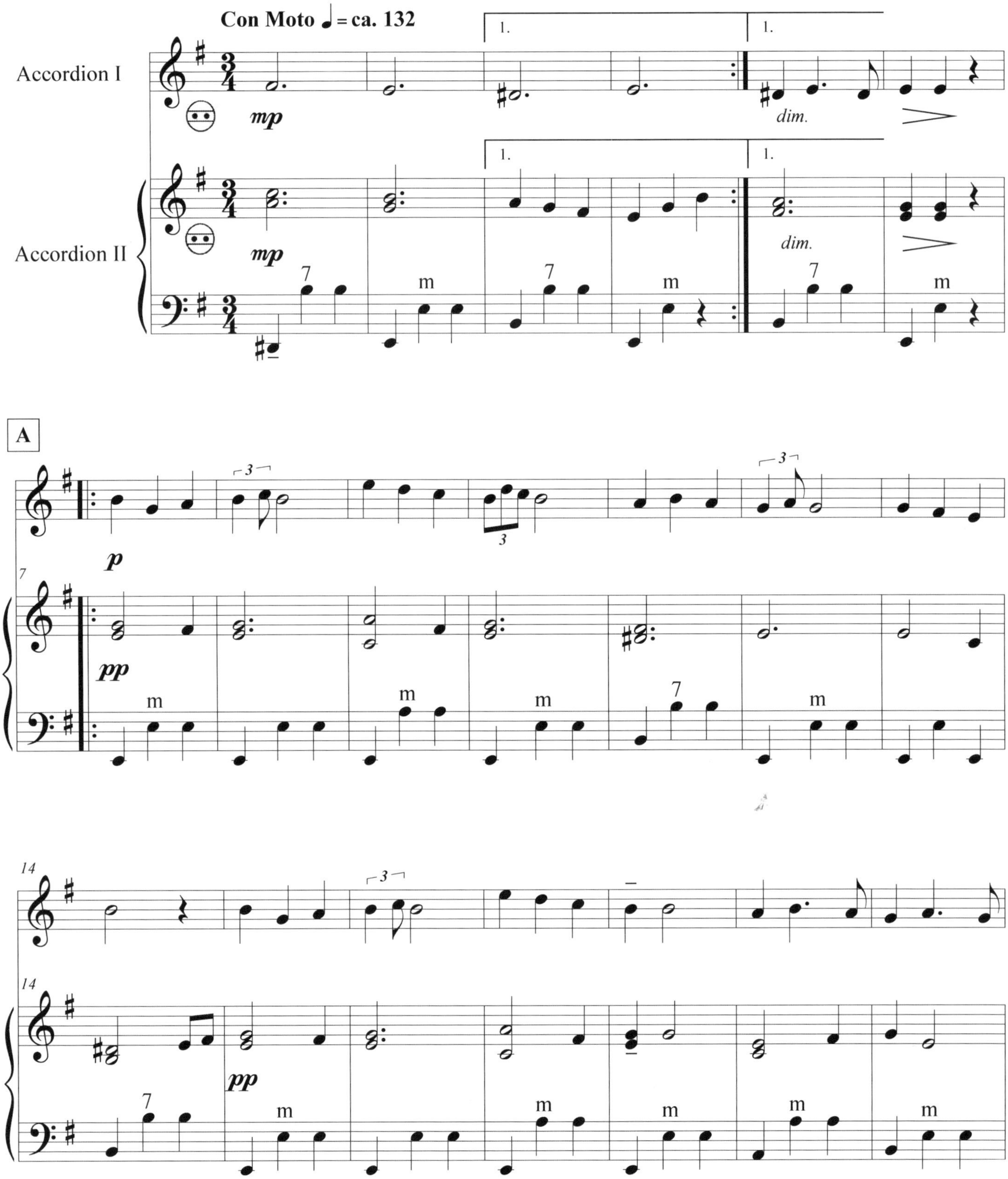

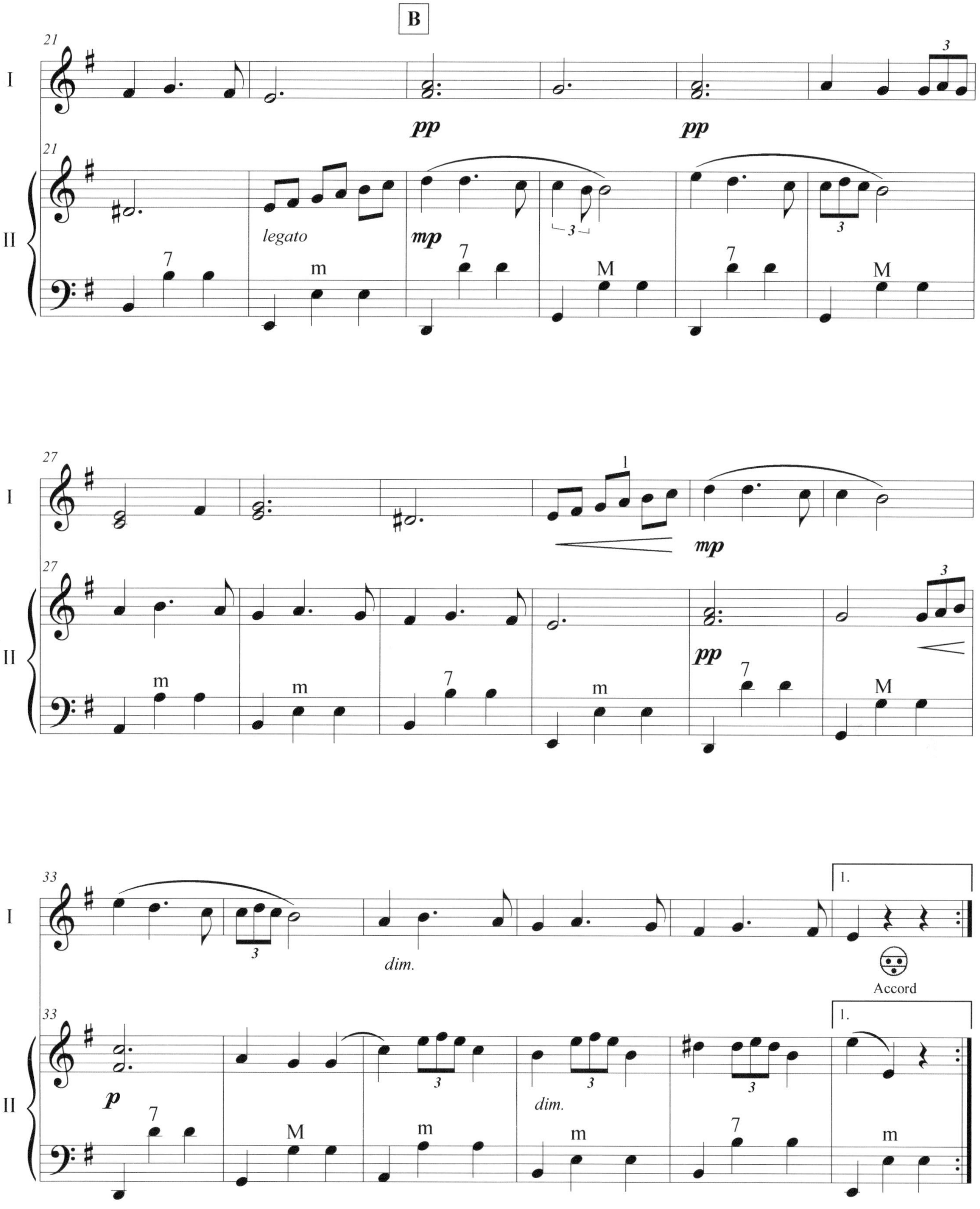
B
I
II
pp
legato
mp
dim.
p
1.
Accord

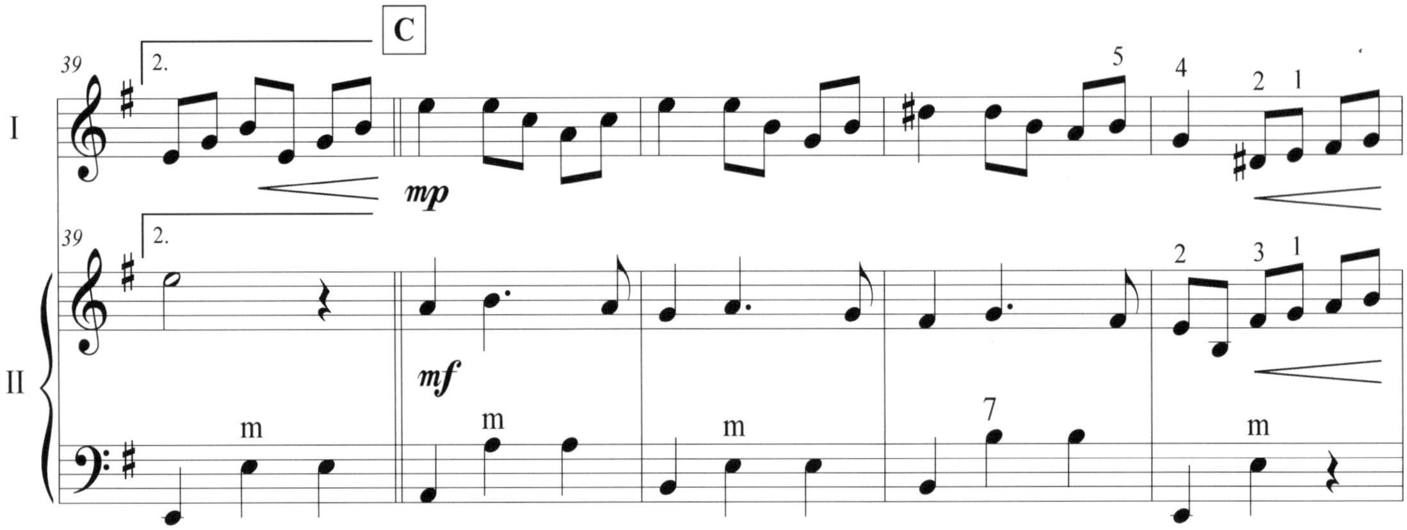
C
2.
I
II
mp
mf
m
7

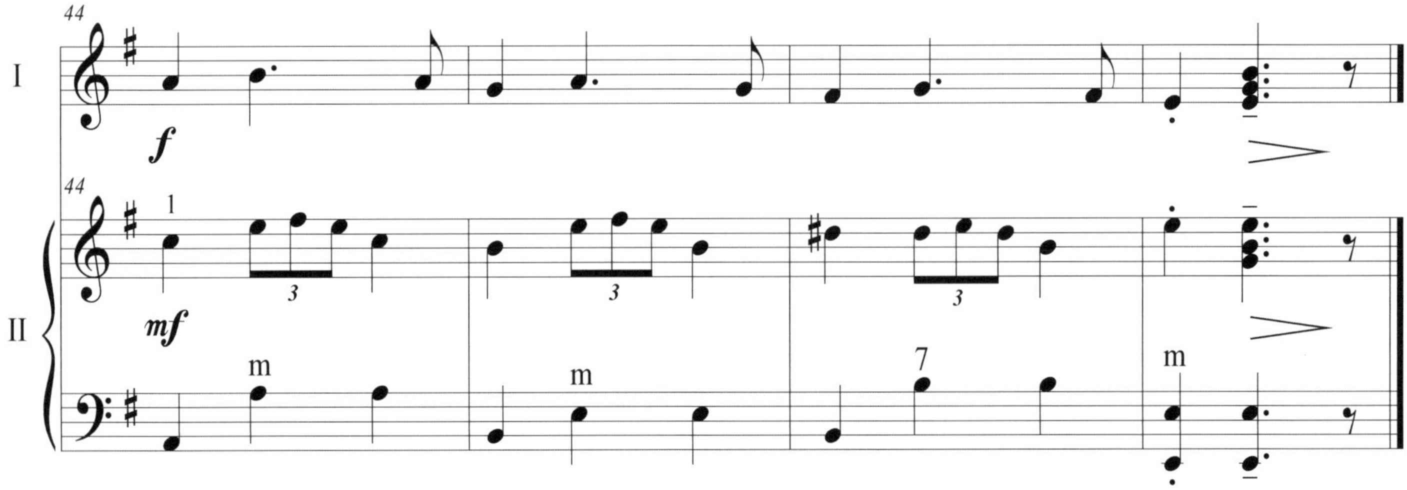
I
II
f
mf
m
7

Canzonettina

Sicilian
Arr. by Carole Gatwood

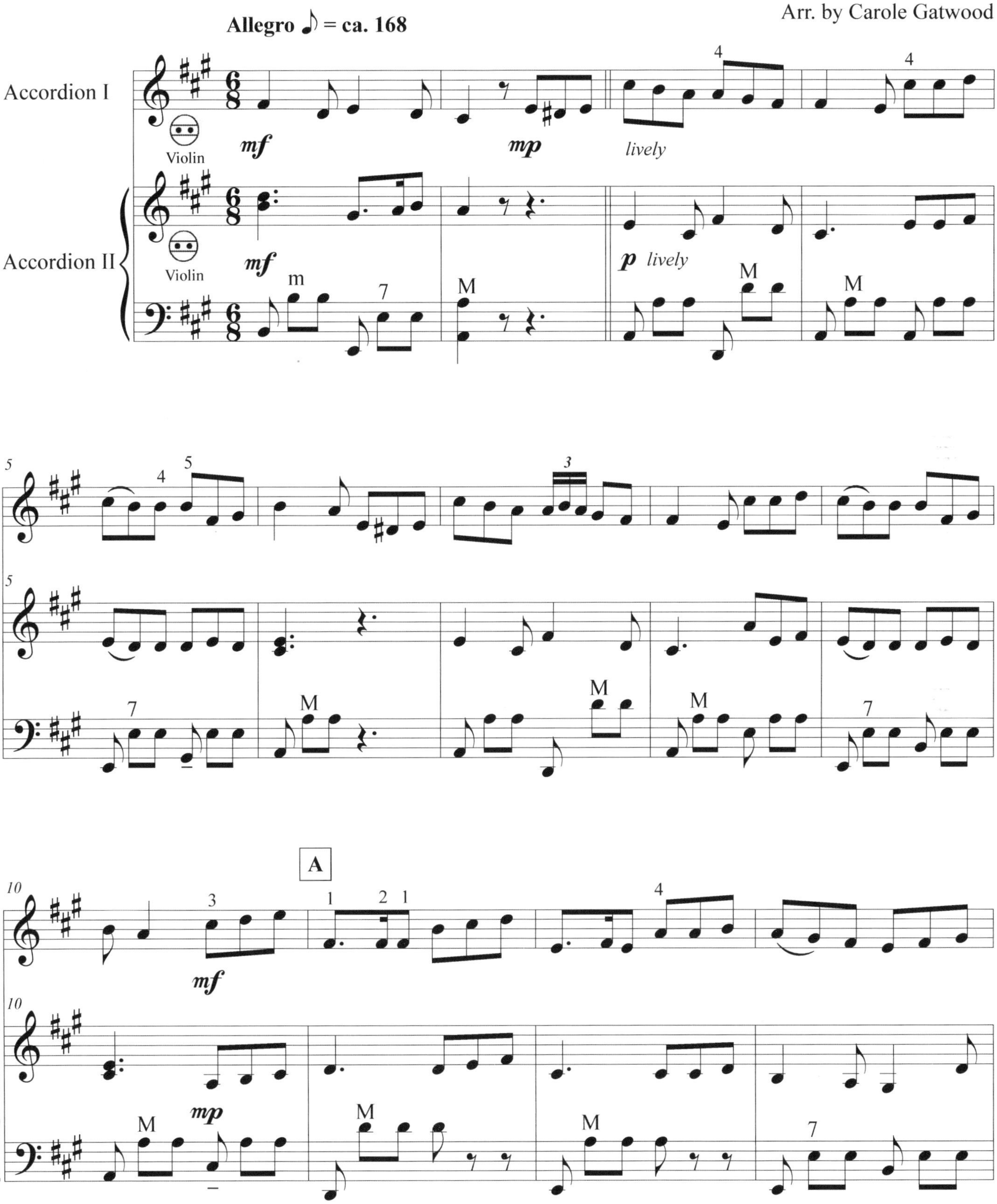

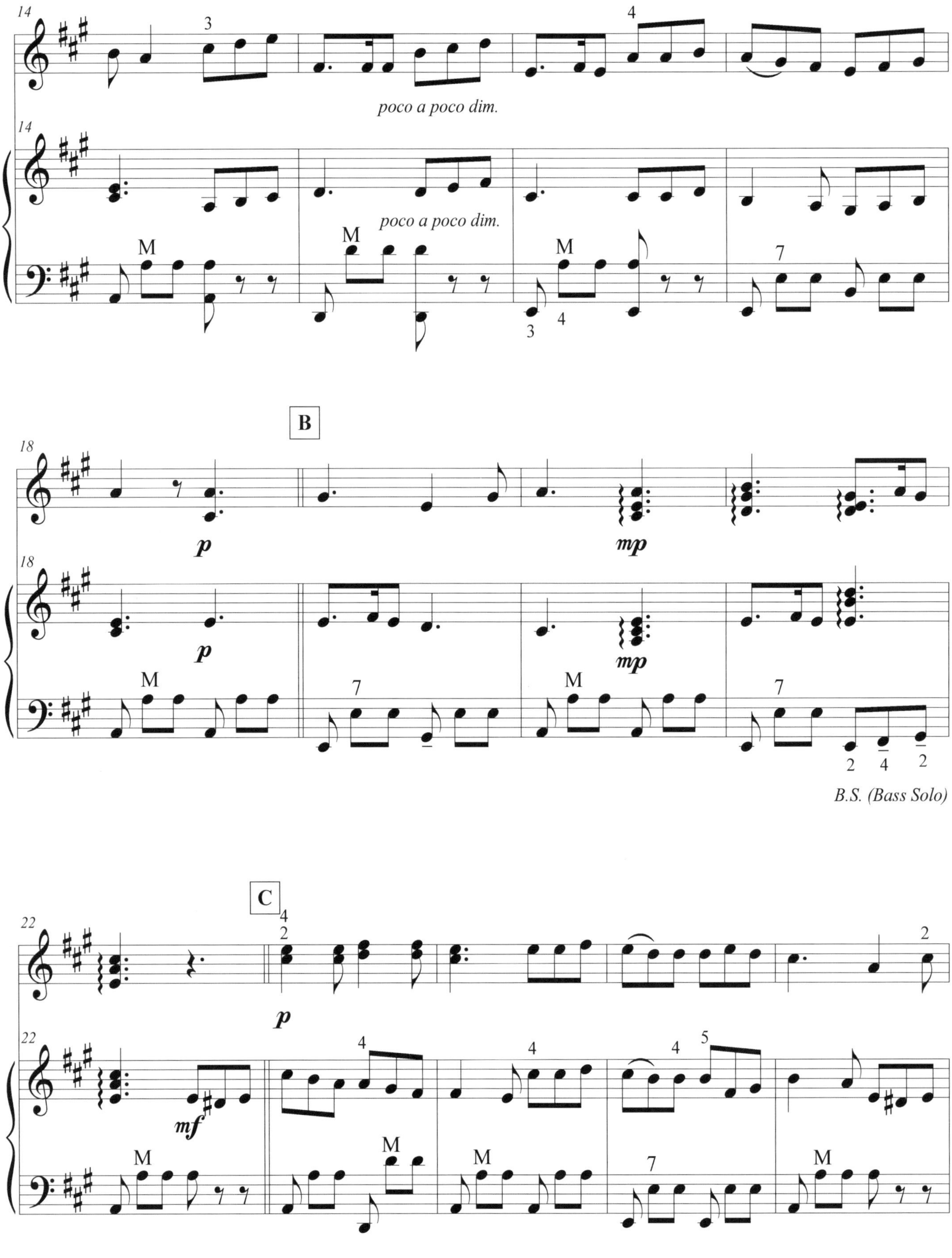
I
II
poco a poco dim.
poco a poco dim.
B
p
p
mp
mp
B.S. (Bass Solo)
C
p
mf

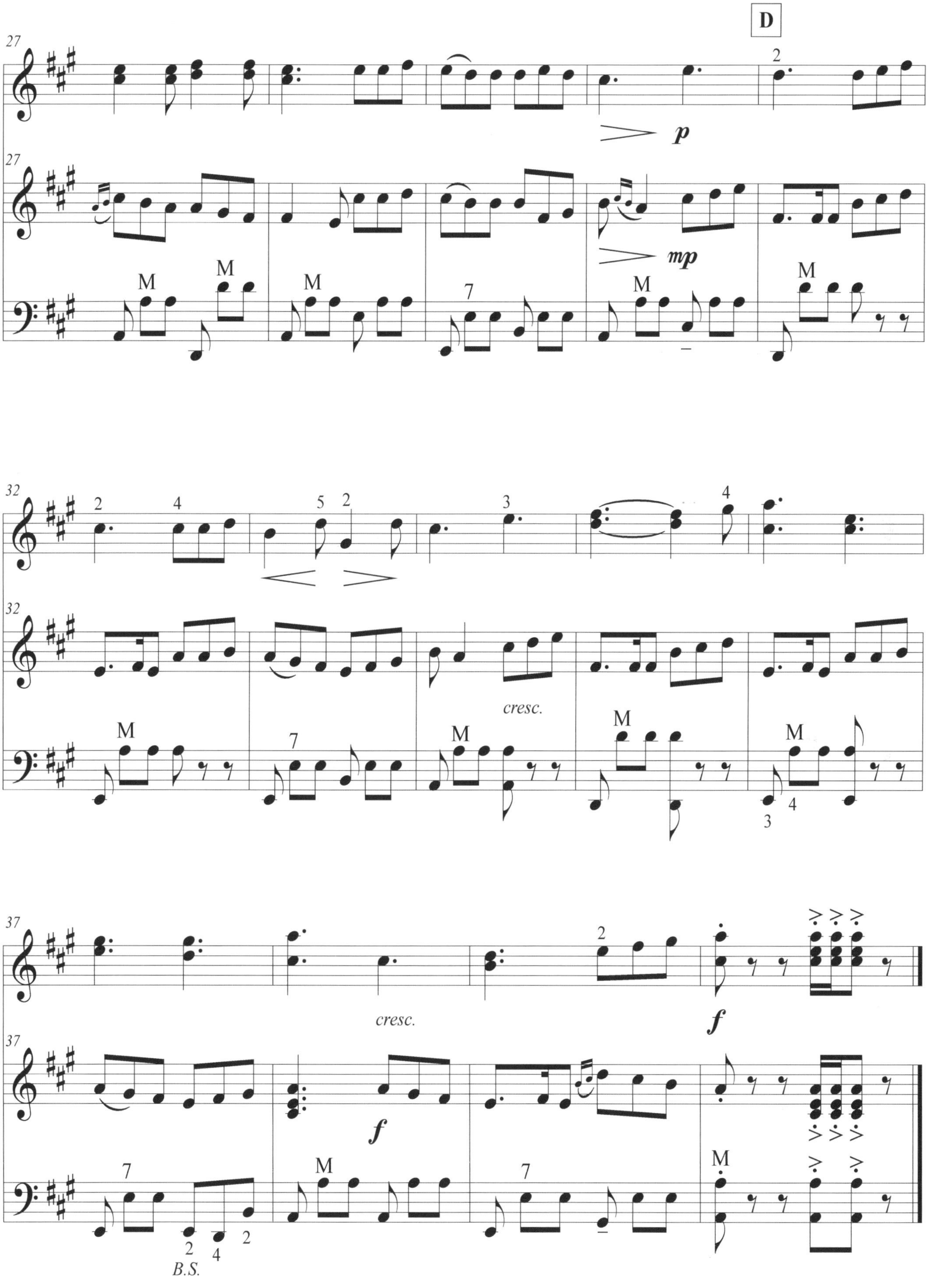
D
I
II
p
mp
cresc.
cresc.
f
f
B.S.

Avvertimento

Canzonetta of Sicily: *A Warning*

Martino Frontini
Arr. by Carole Gatwood

Andantino grazioso ♩ = 84 - 88

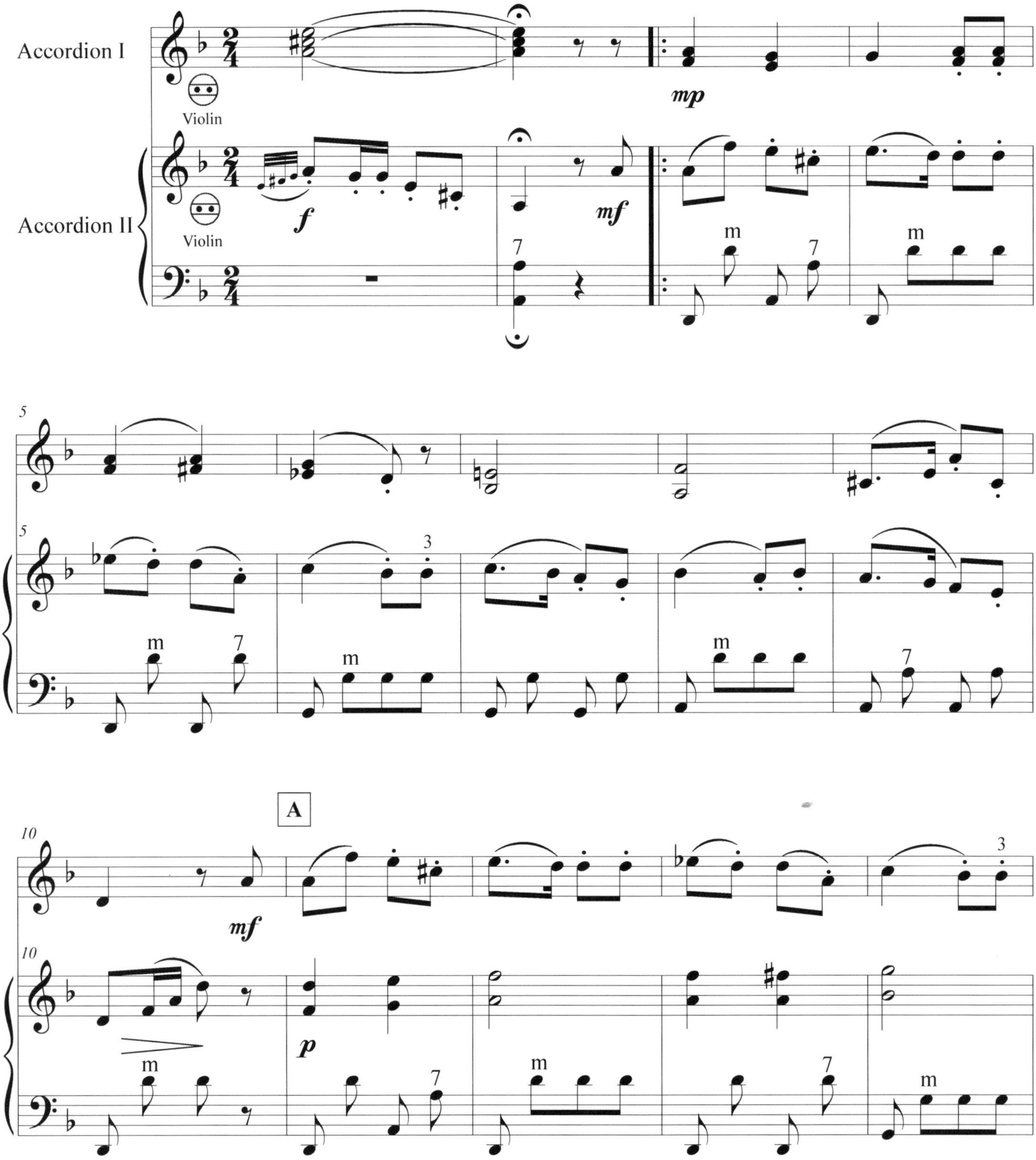

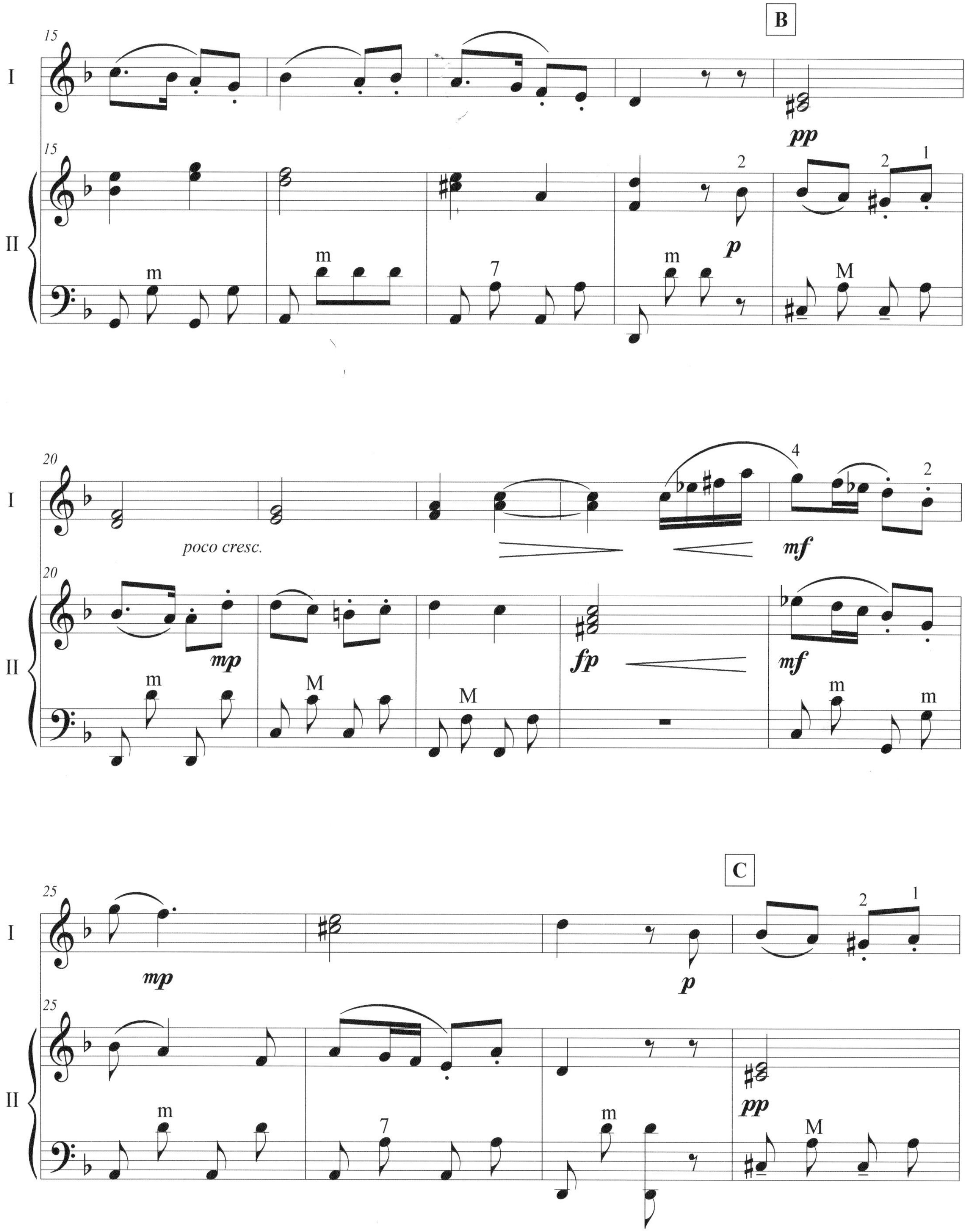
B
I
II
pp
p
poco cresc.
mf
mp
fp
C

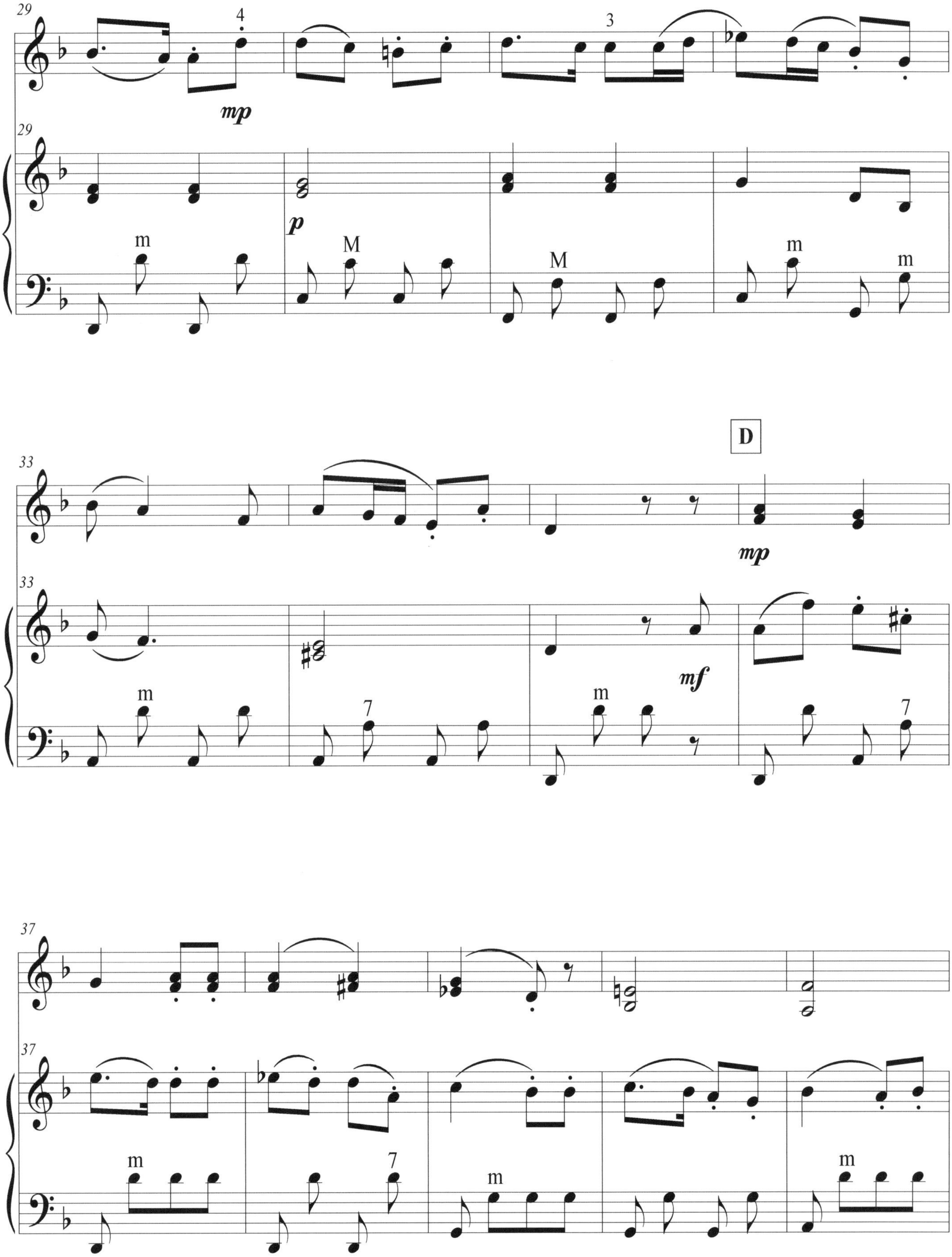
I
II
mp
p
mf
D
m
M
7

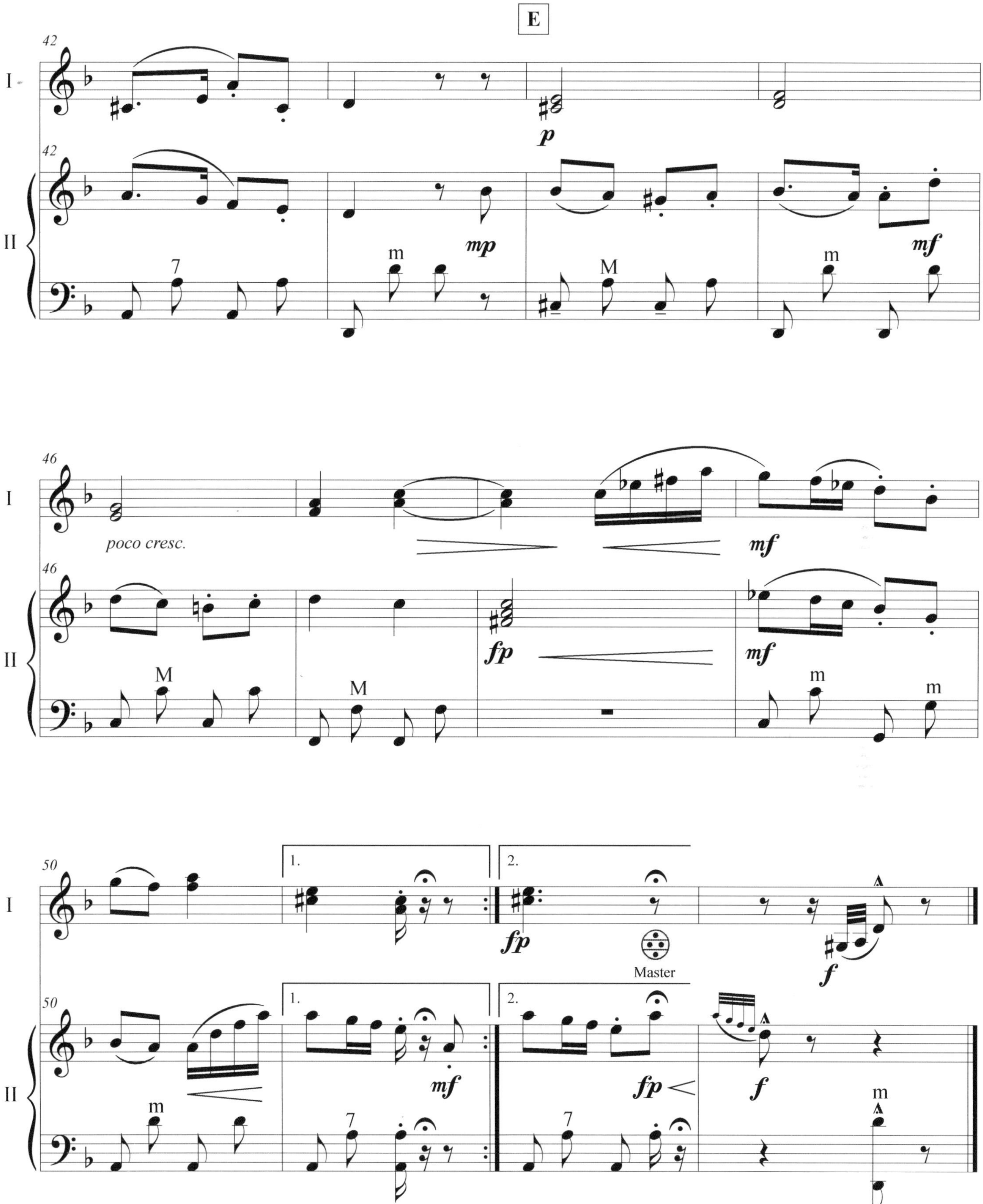
E
I
II
poco cresc.
1.
2.
Master

La Fata d'Amalfi

Serenade of Amalfi Boatmen

Teodoro Cottrau
Arr. by Carole Gatwood

Andantino (♪ = ca. 138)

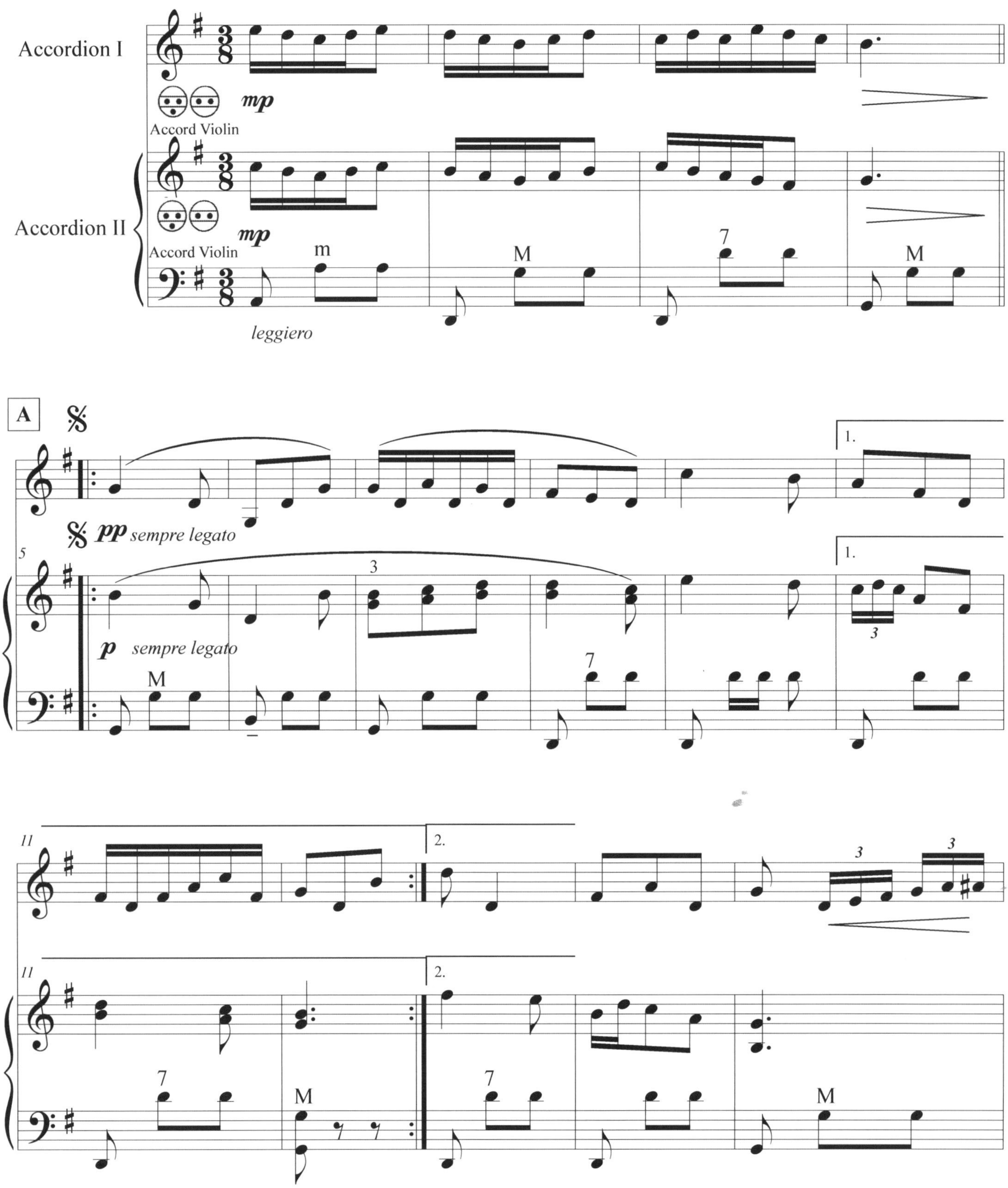

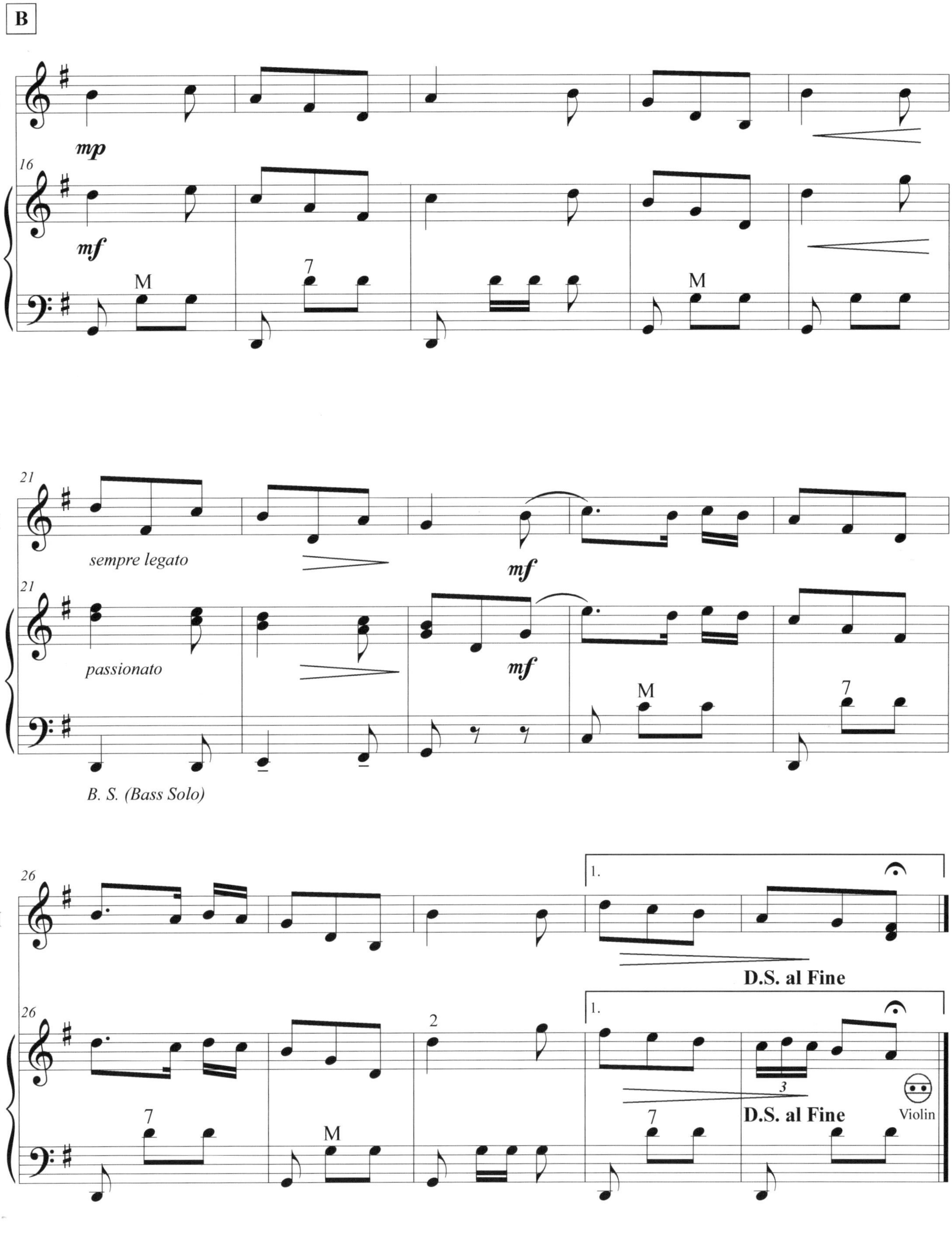
B
I
II
mp
mf
M
7
sempre legato
passionato
B. S. (Bass Solo)
1.
D.S. al Fine
2
Violin

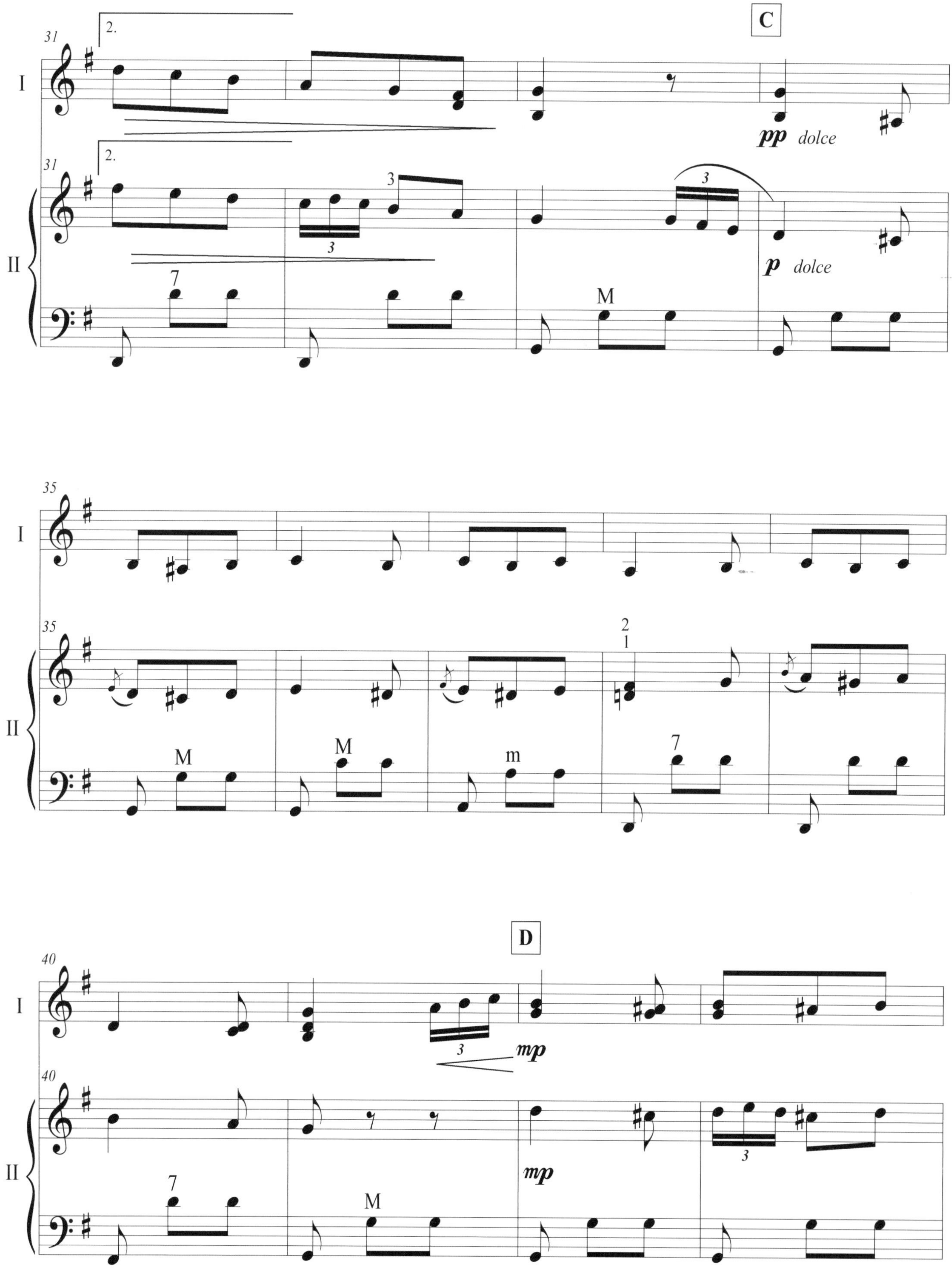
C
2.
I
II
pp dolce
p dolce
D
mp

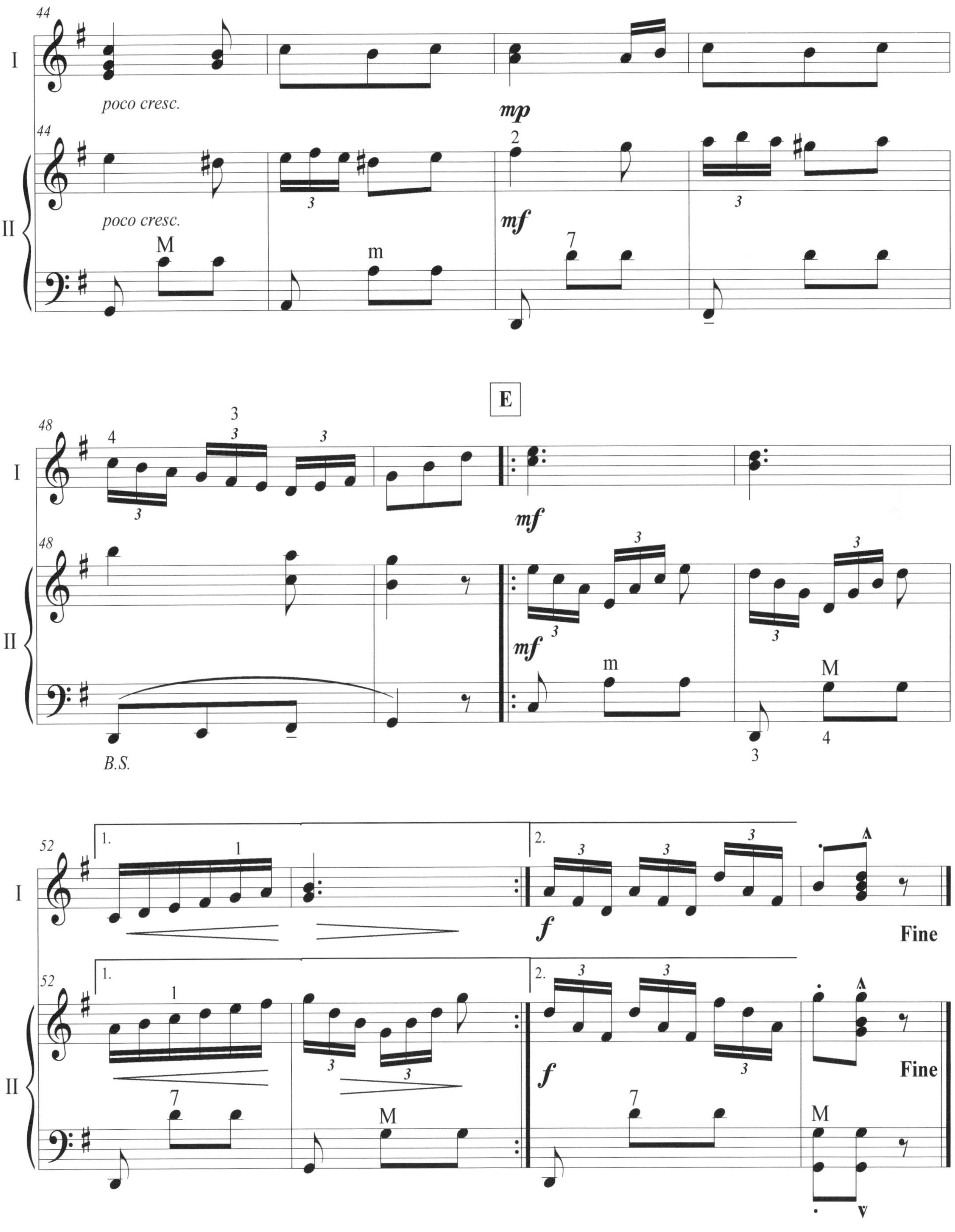
I
II
poco cresc.
poco cresc.
M
m
mp
mf
E
mf
mf
m
M
B.S.
1.
2.
f
f
Fine
Fine

L'Agnesina

Canzonetta di Napoli

Guglielmo Cottrau
Arr. by Carole Gatwood

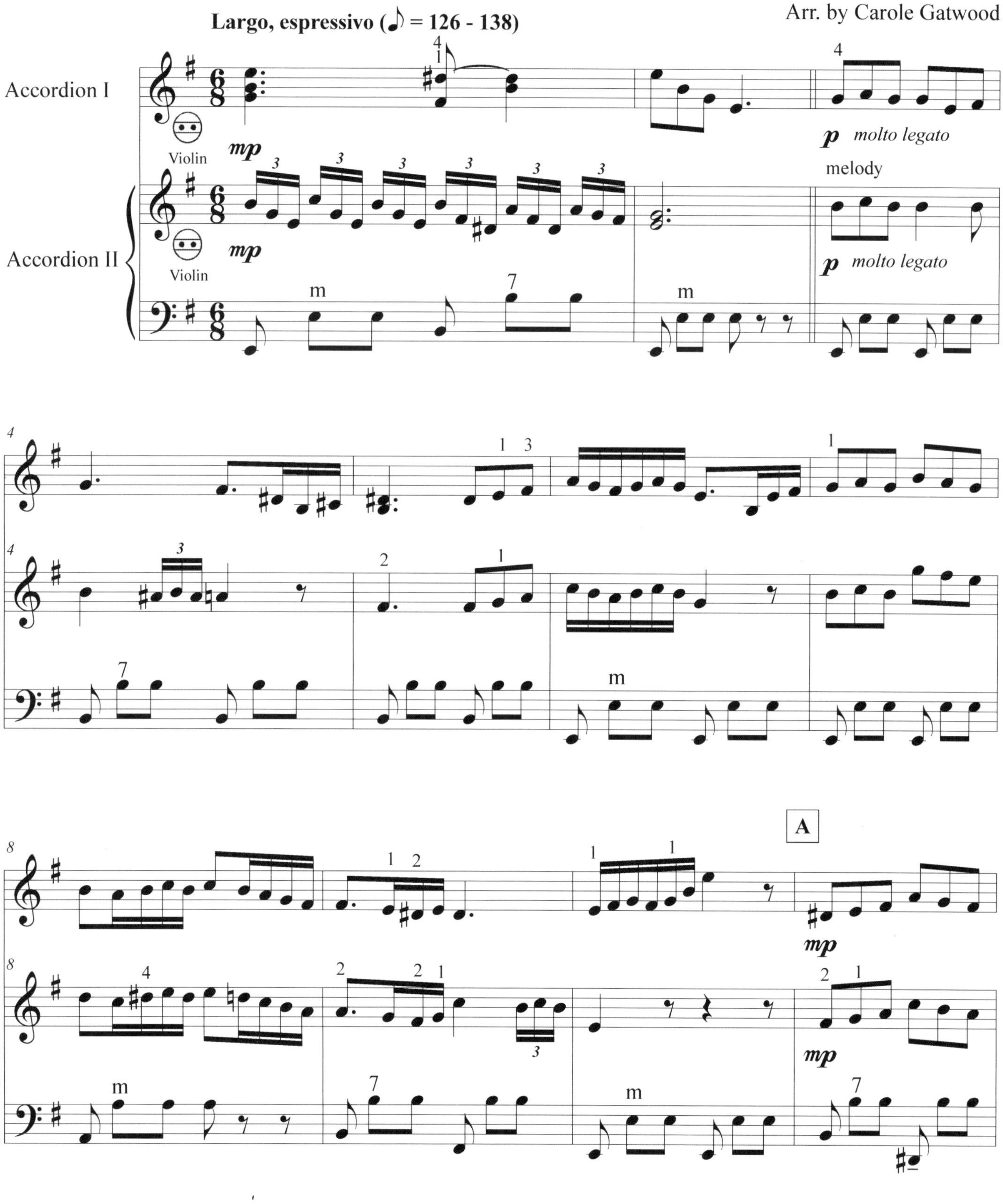

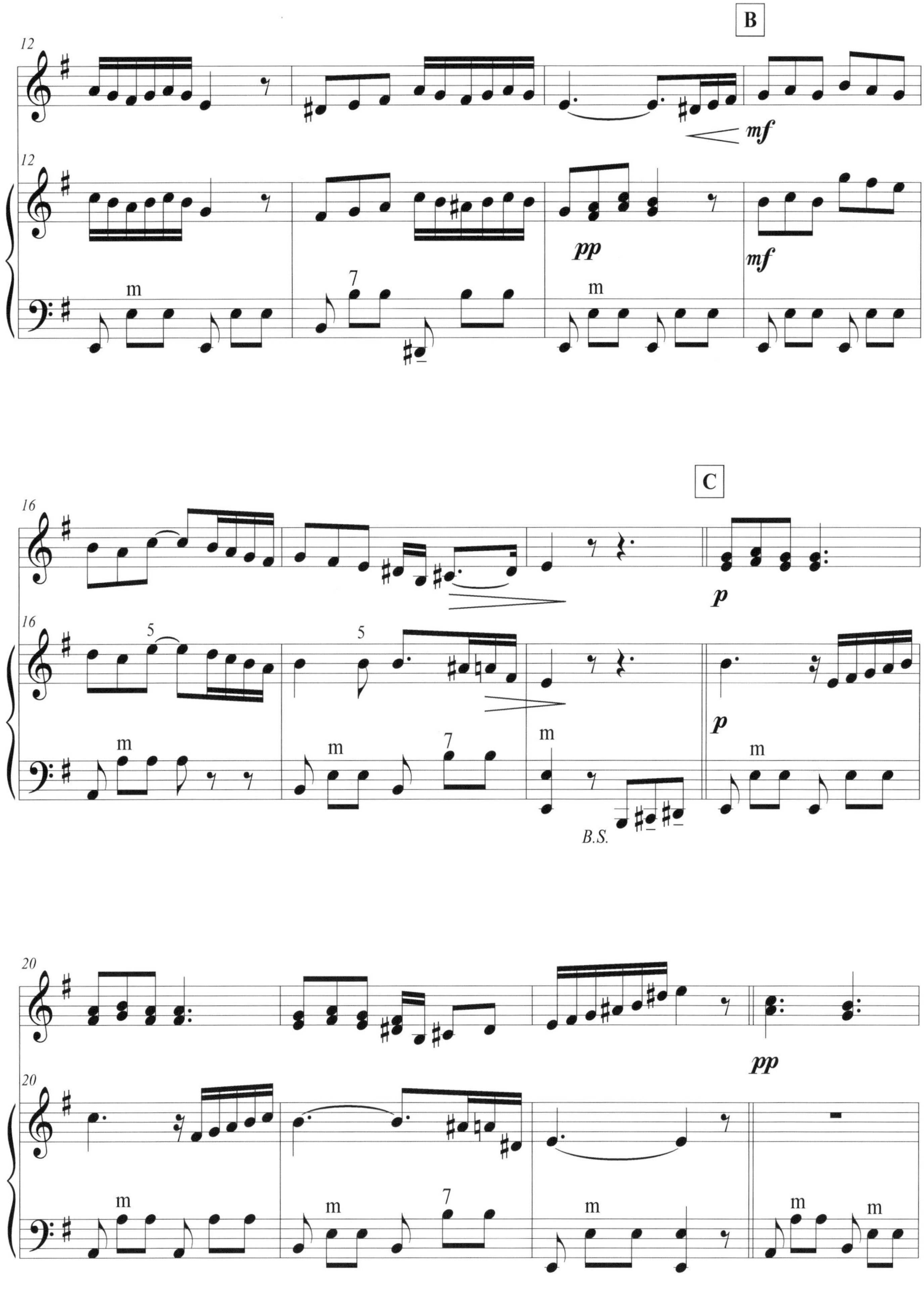
B
I
II
C
B.S.

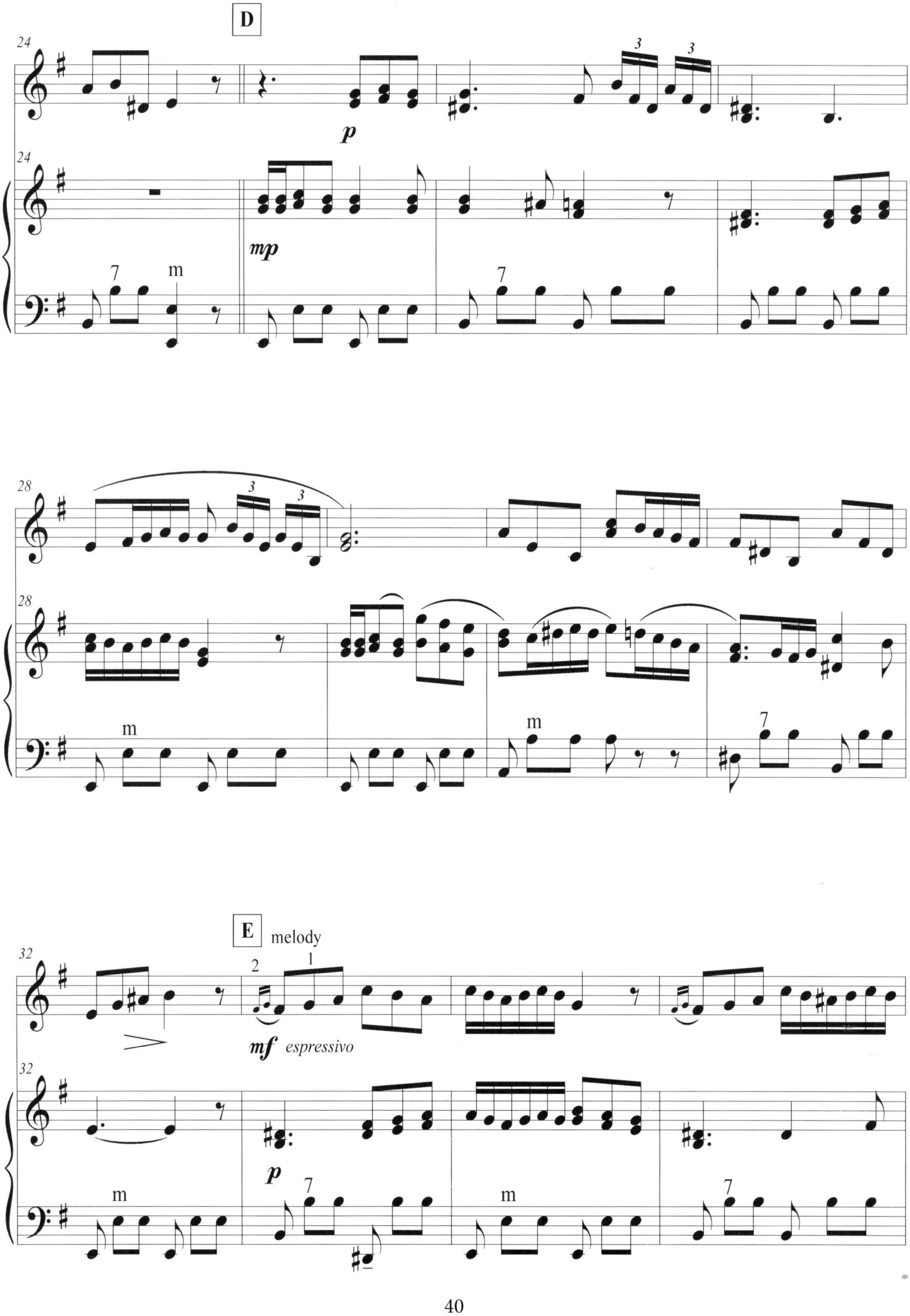
D
I
II
E
melody
mf espressivo

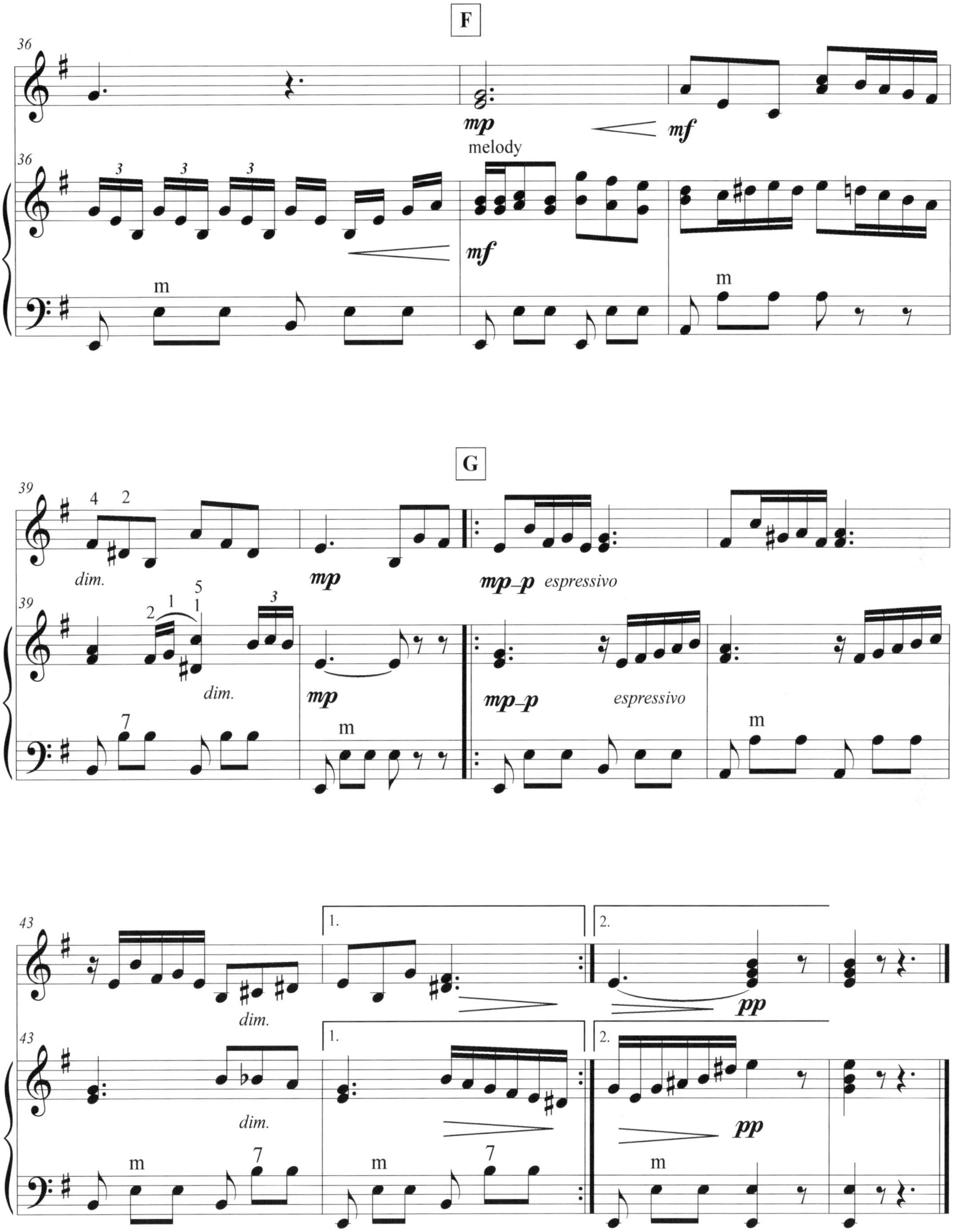
F
36
I
mp
mf
melody
II
m
G
39
4 2
dim.
mp
mp_p espressivo
espressivo
7
43
1.
2.
pp

La Marinarella

Guglielmo Cottrau
Arr. by Carole Gatwood

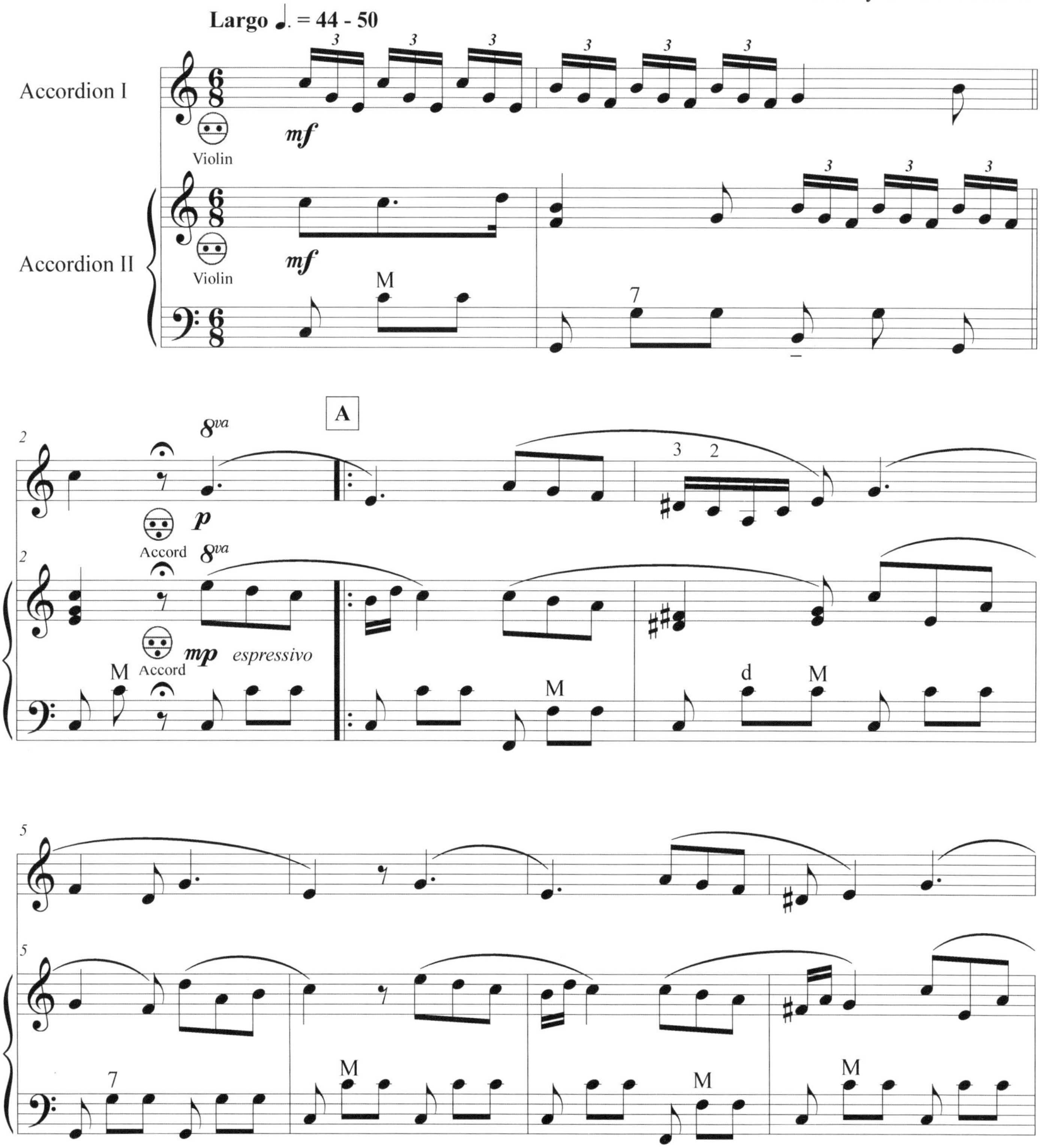

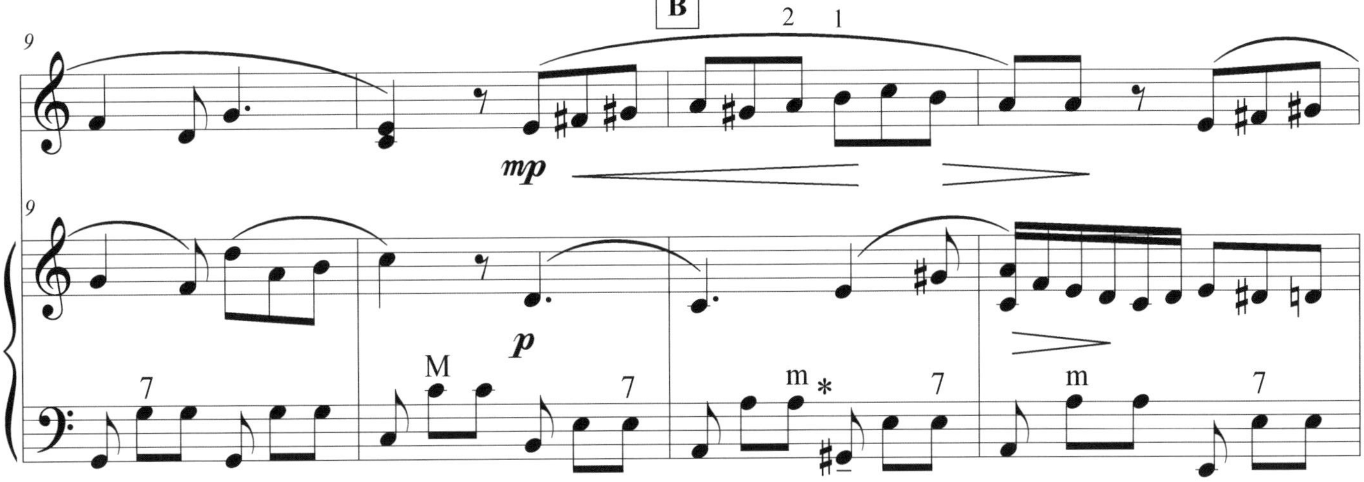

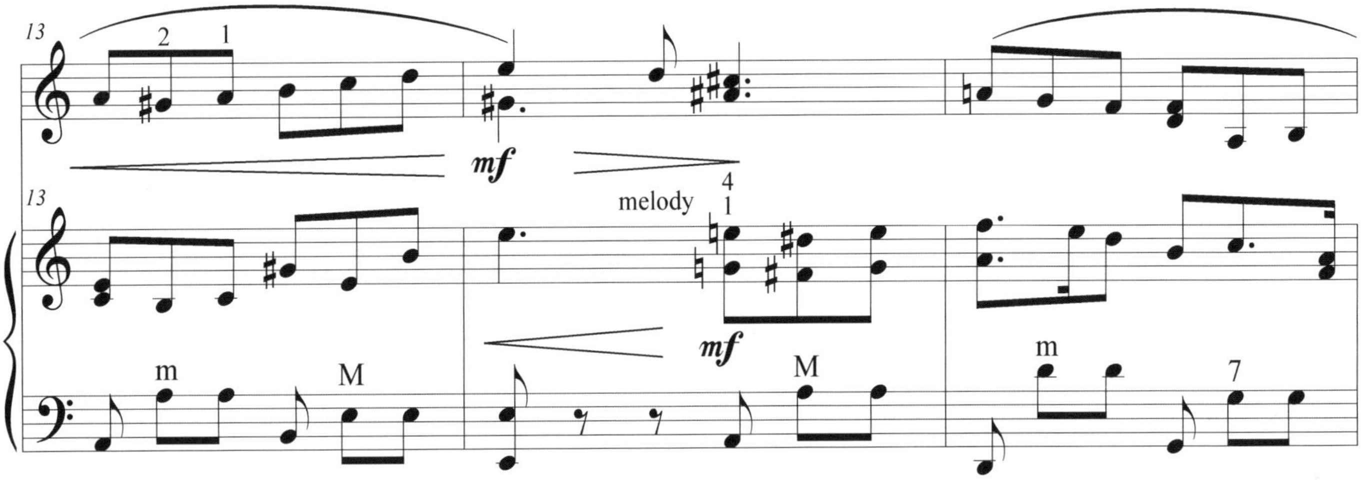

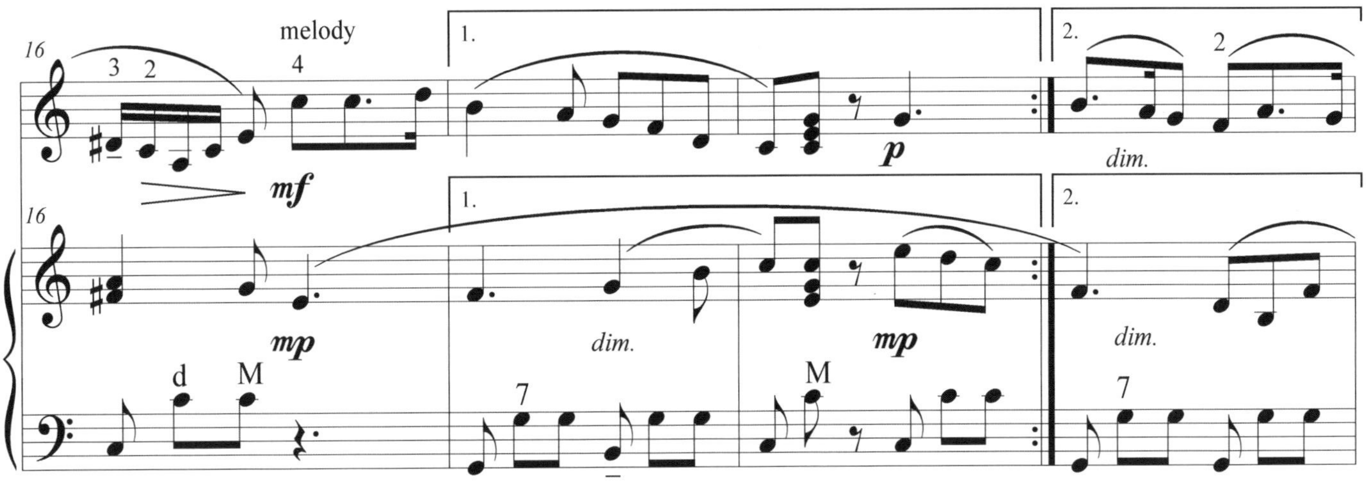

* In the second half of measures 11 and 21, E bass & E7 chord may be played.

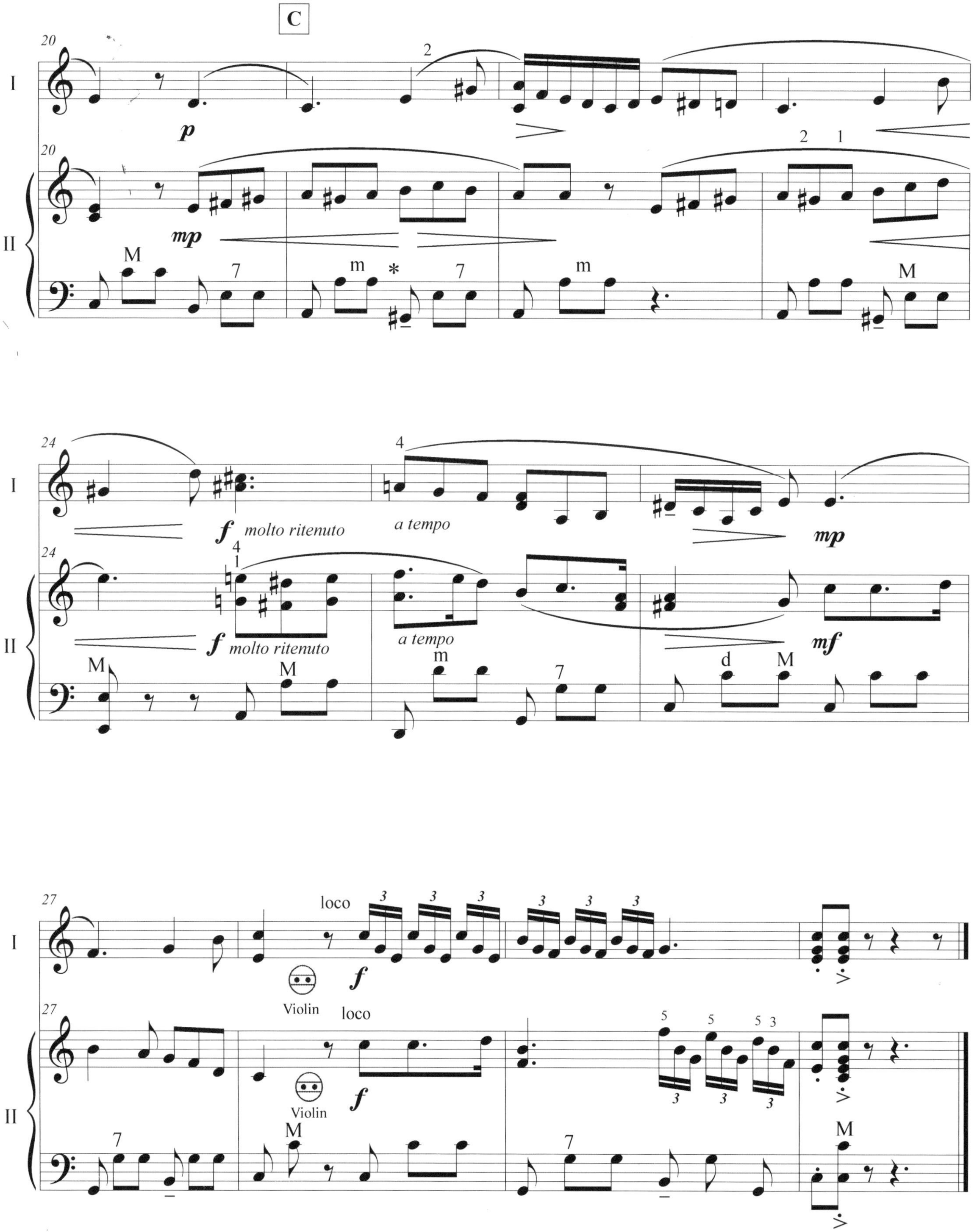
C
I
II
p
mp
molto ritenuto
a tempo
mf
loco
Violin

Canzonetta Popolare Nella Vendemmia

The Grape Harvest

Sicilian
Arr. by Carole Gatwood

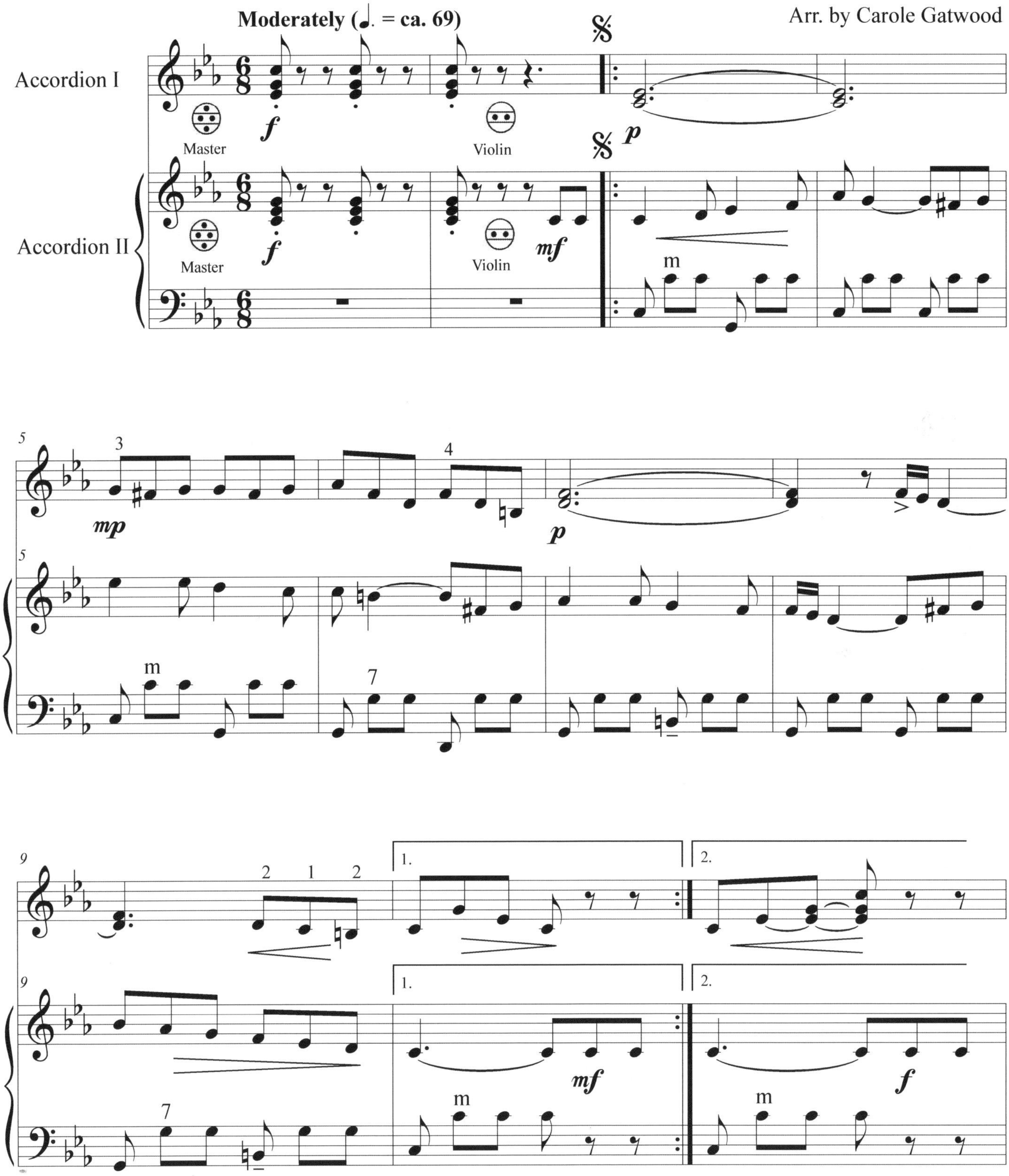

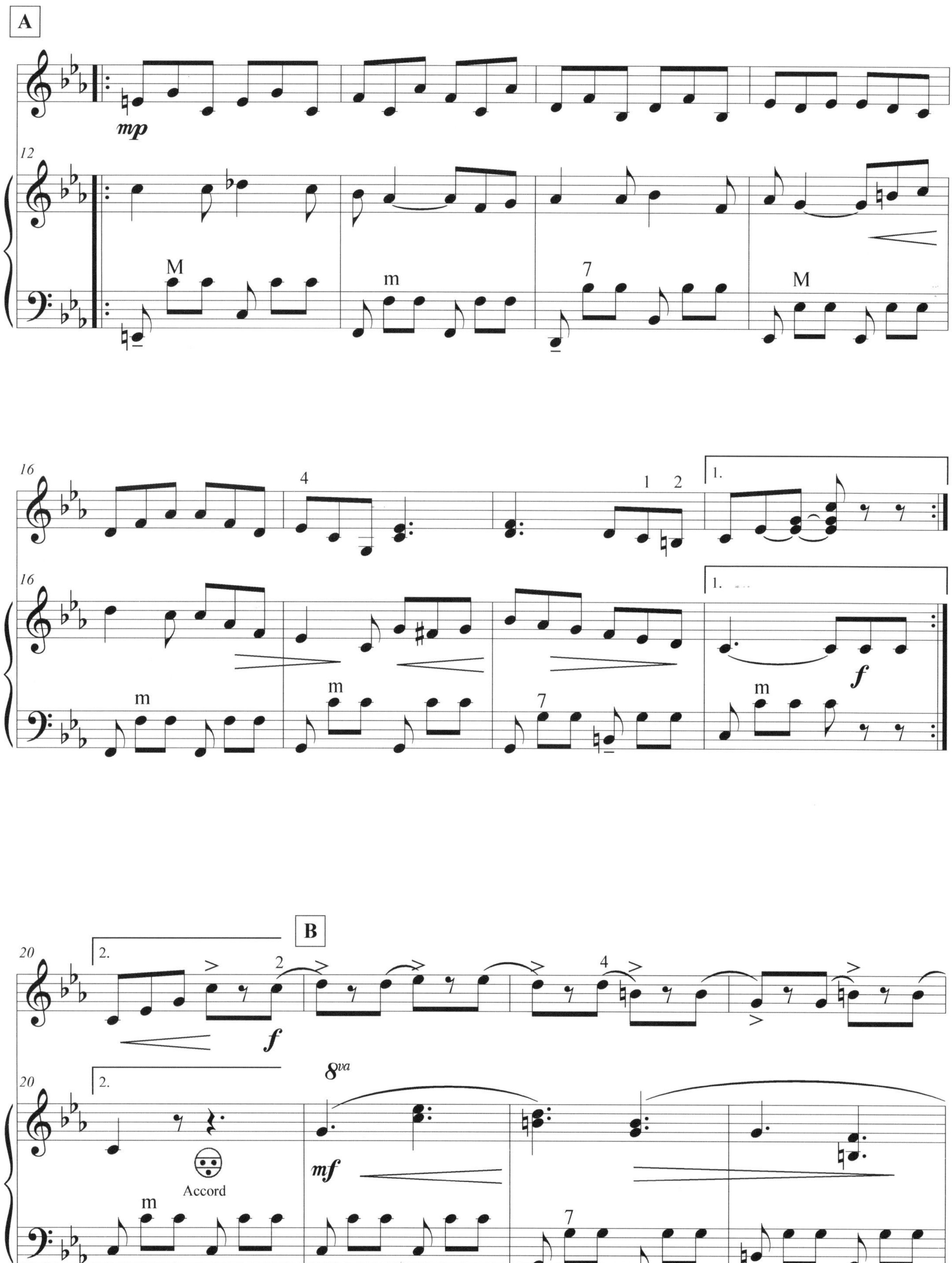
A
I
mp
12
II
M
m
7
M
16
I
4
1 2
1.
16
II
m
m
7
1.
m
f
B
20
I
2.
2
f
4
20
2.
8va
II
Accord
mf
m
7

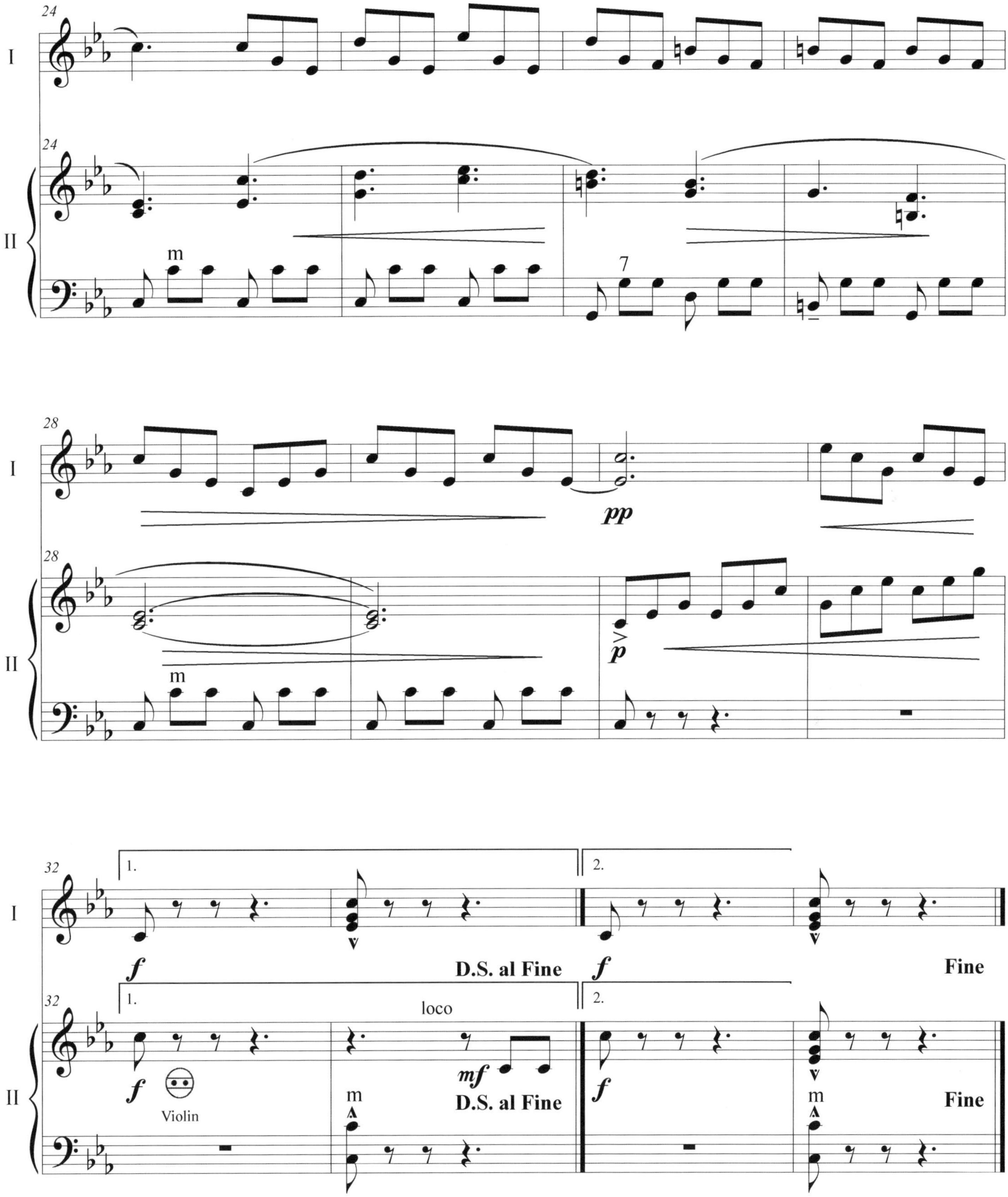
24
I
II
m
7
28
pp
p
32
1.
2.
f
D.S. al Fine
Fine
loco
mf
Violin

Un Mazzo di Fiori

"a bouquet of flowers"

Neopolitan Folk Song
Arr. by Carole Gatwood

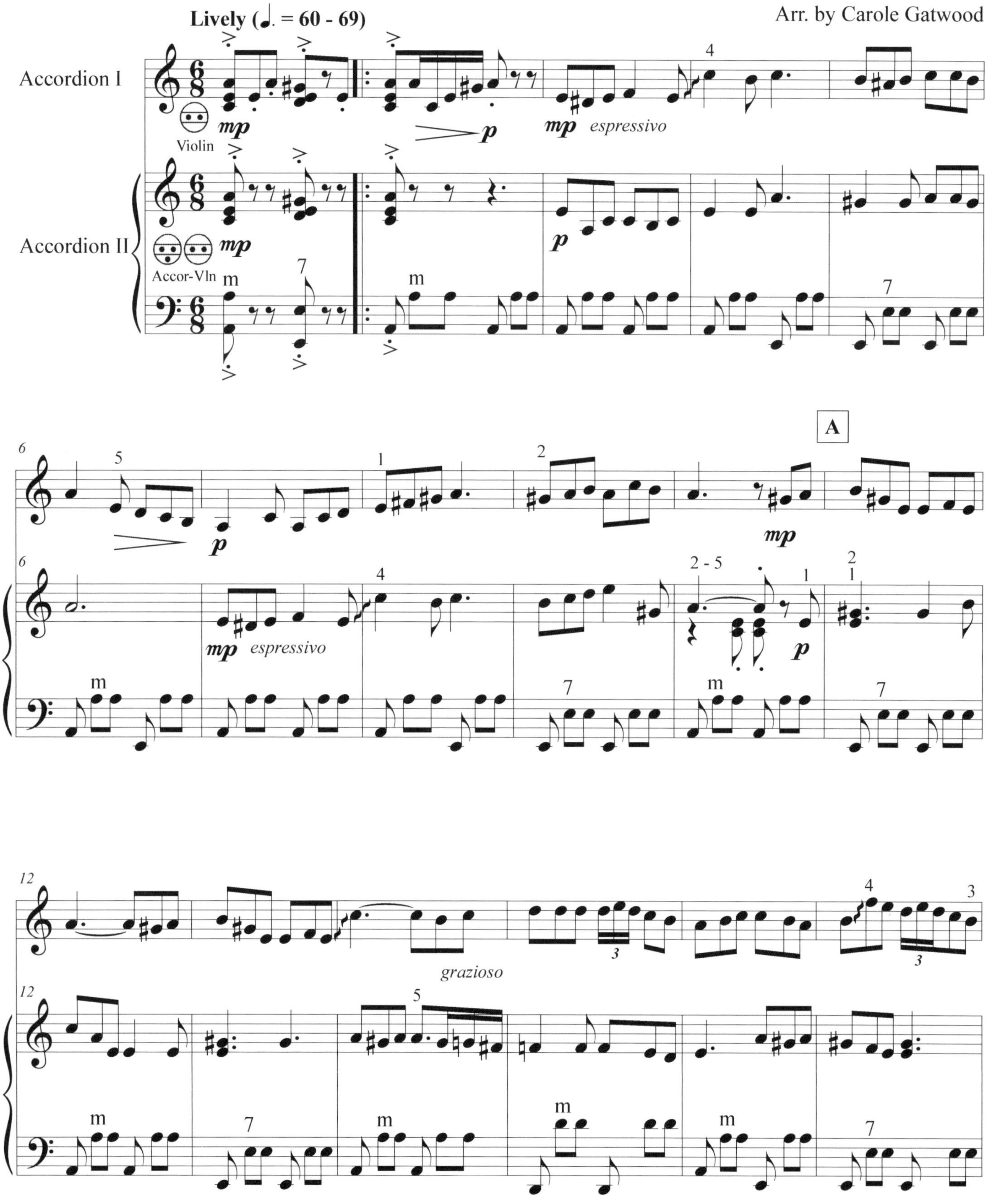

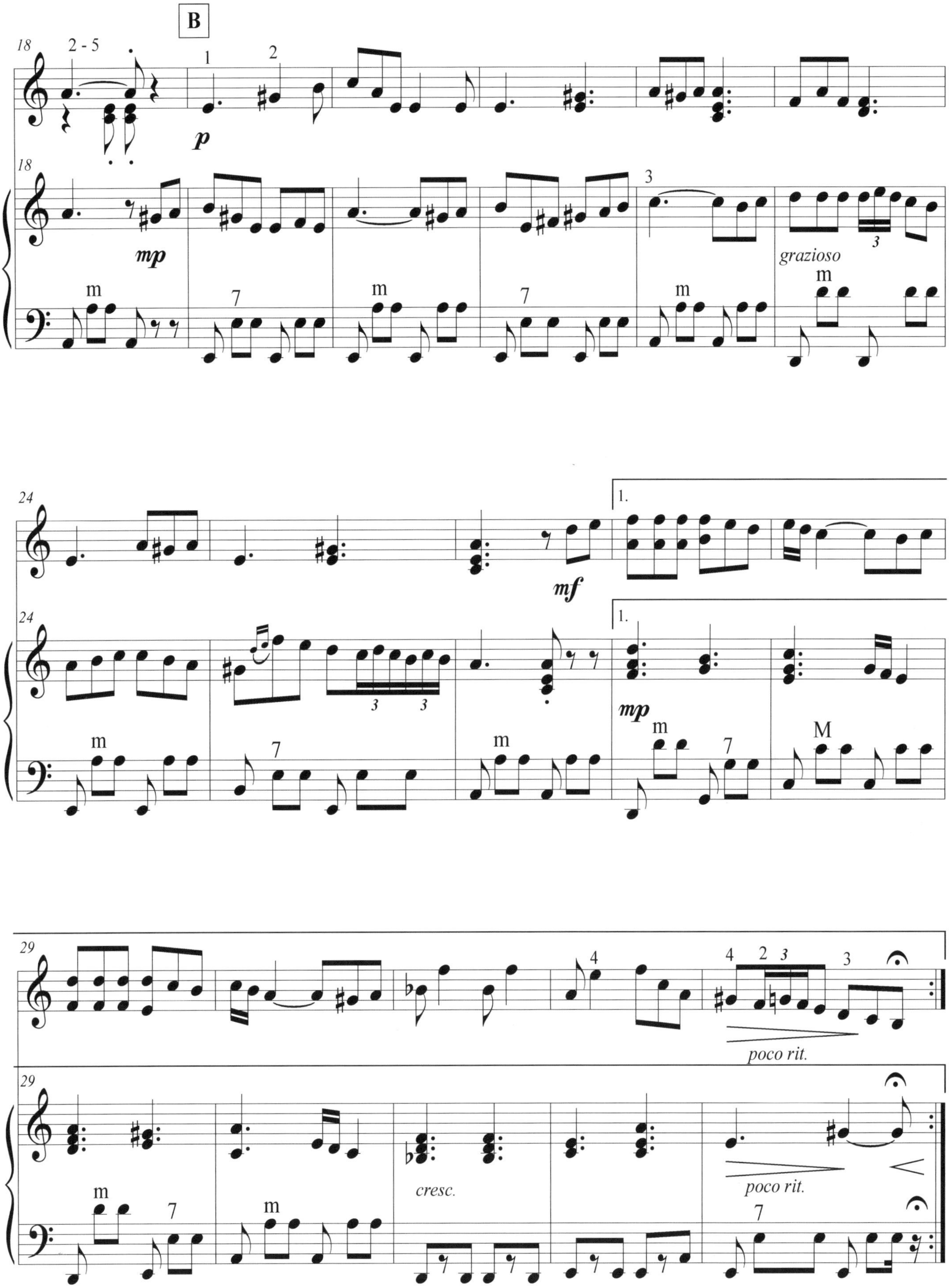

B.S.

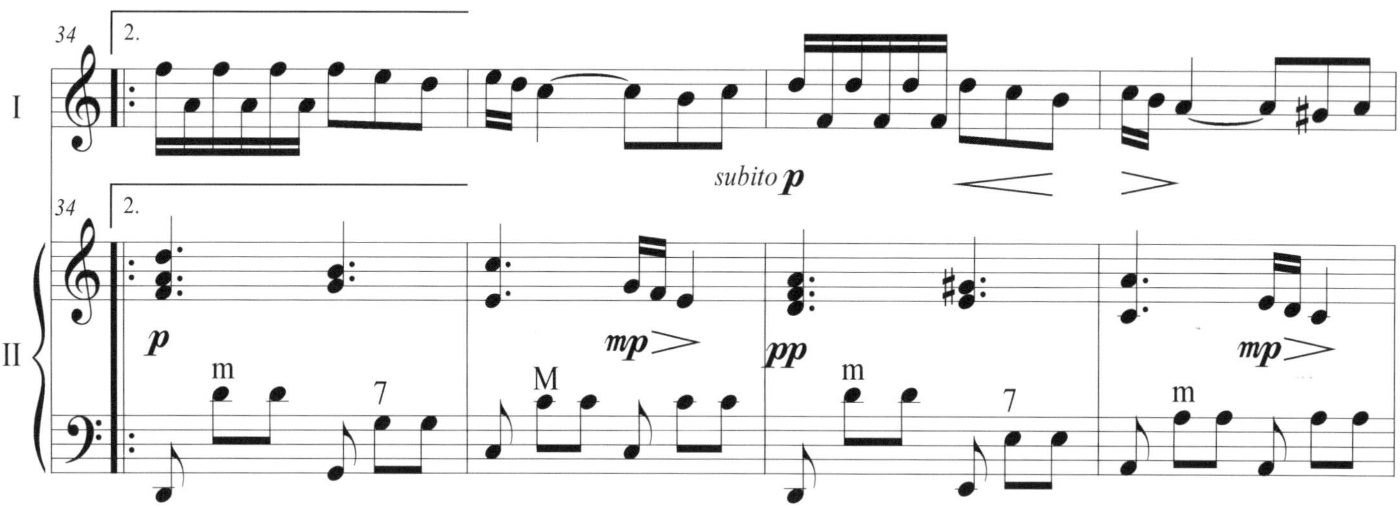
I
II
subito p
mp
pp

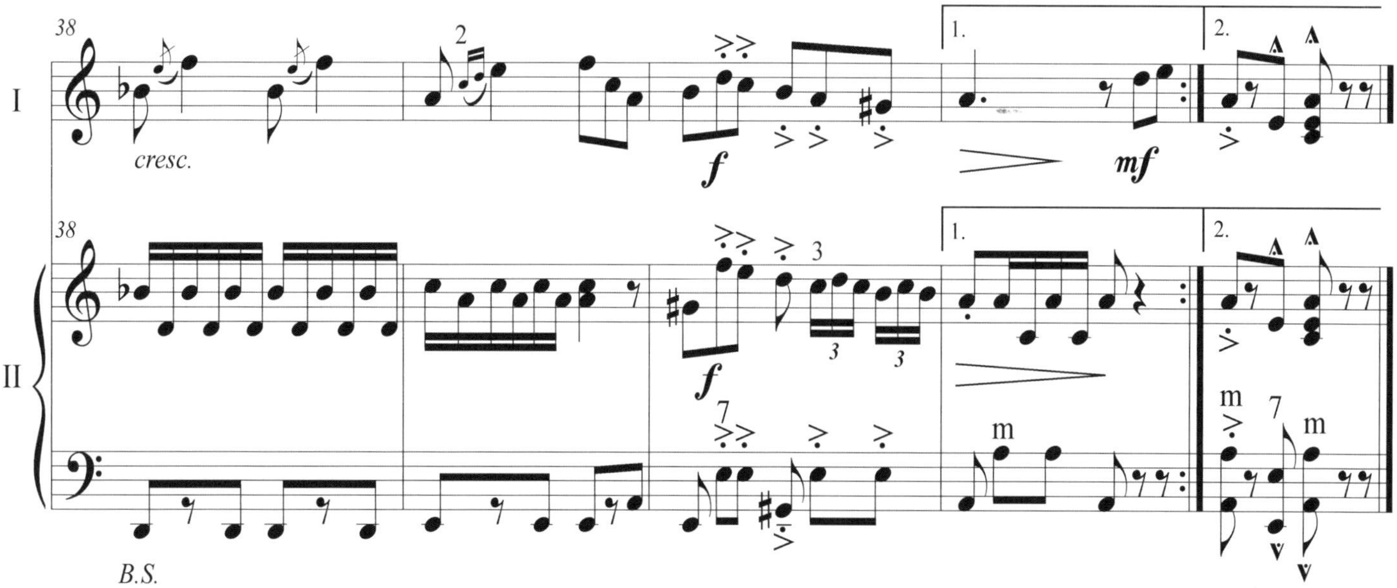
I
II
cresc.
f
mf
B.S.

This page has been left blank to avoid an awkward page turn.

Santa Lucia

Neapolitan
Arr. by Carole Gatwood

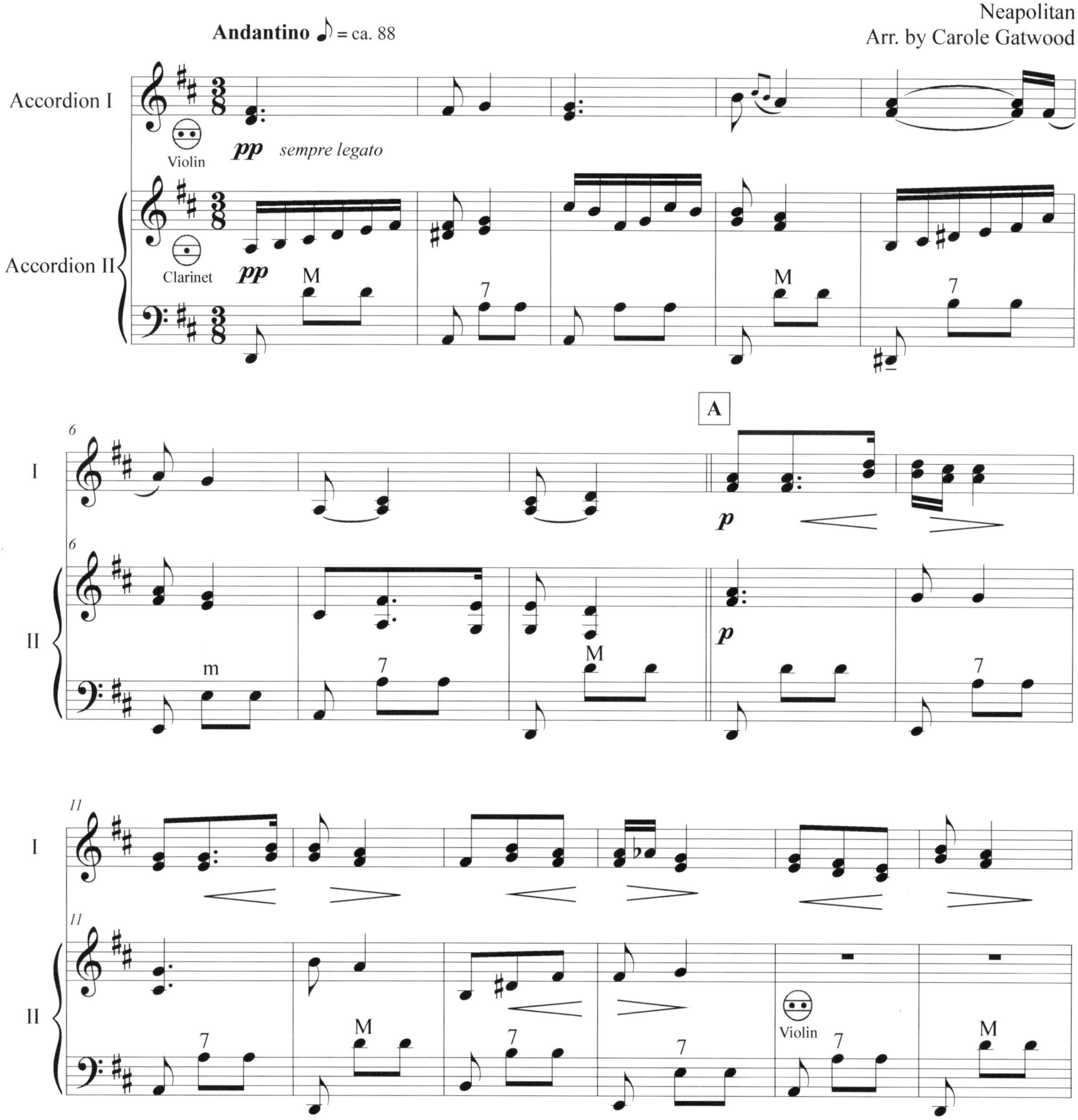

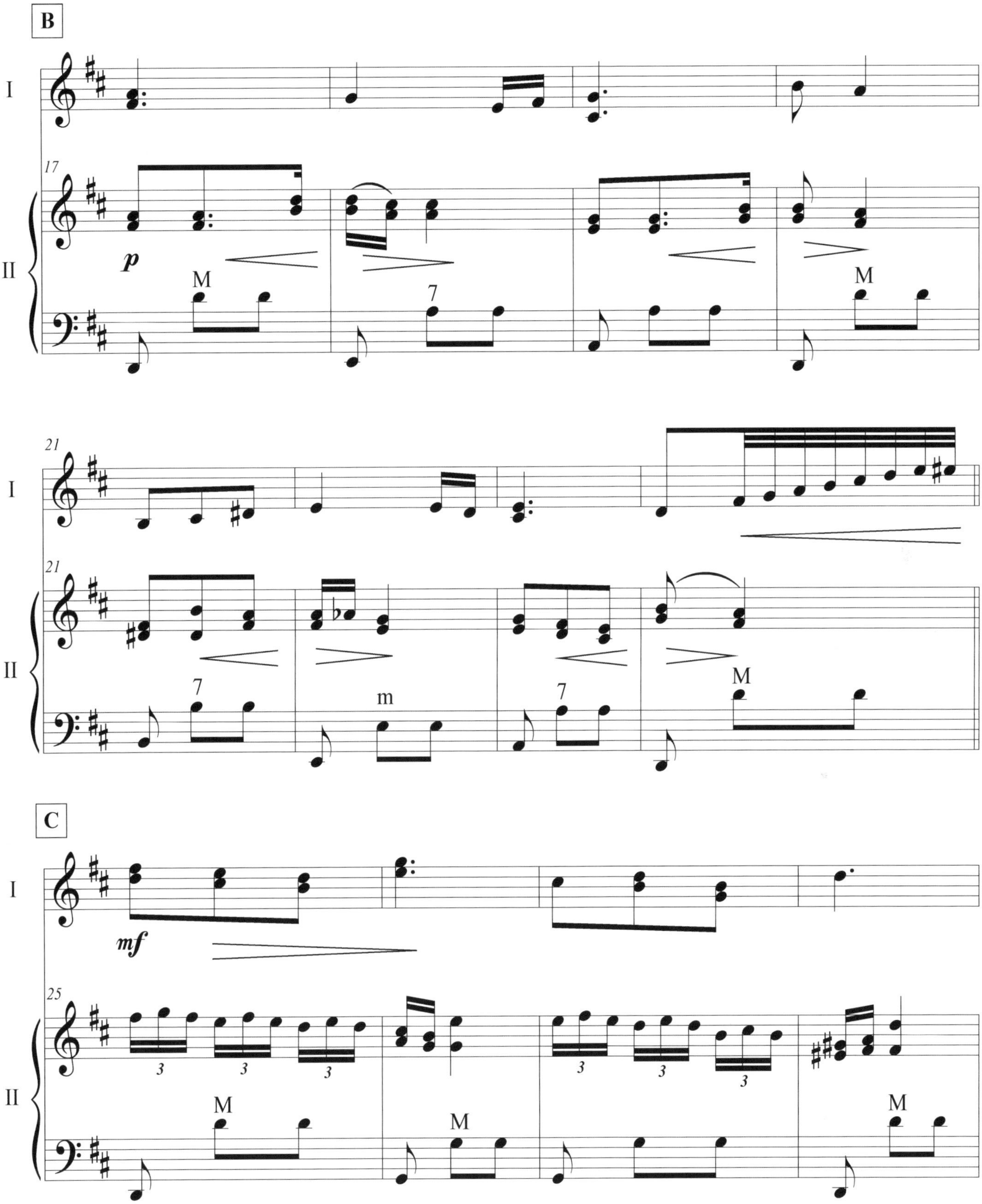
B
I
II
17
p
M
7
M
21
I
21
II
7
m
7
M
C
I
mf
25
II
3
M
M
M

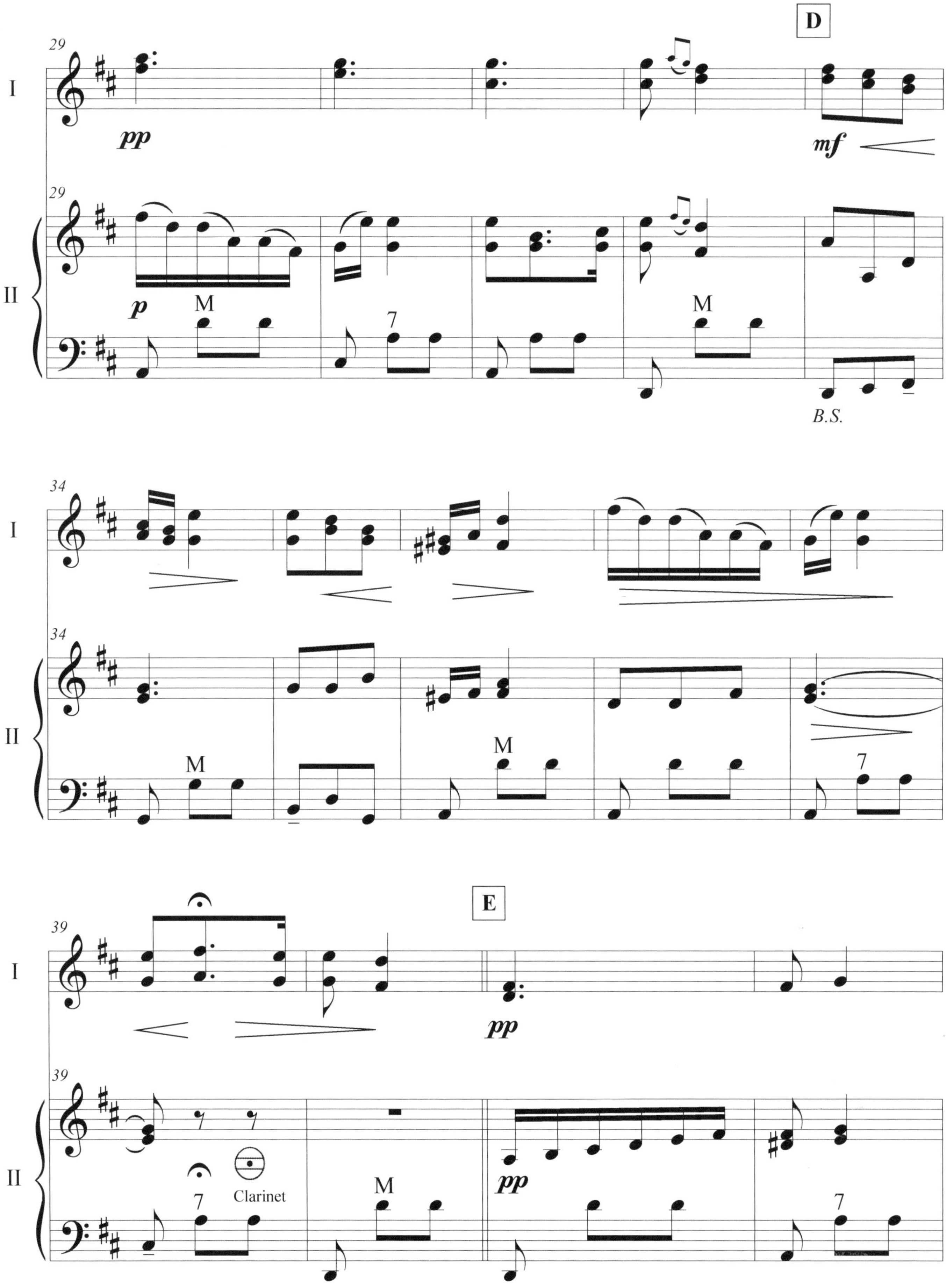
D
29
I
pp
mf
29
II
p
M
7
M
B.S.
34
I
34
II
M
M
7
E
39
I
pp
39
II
7
Clarinet
M
pp
7

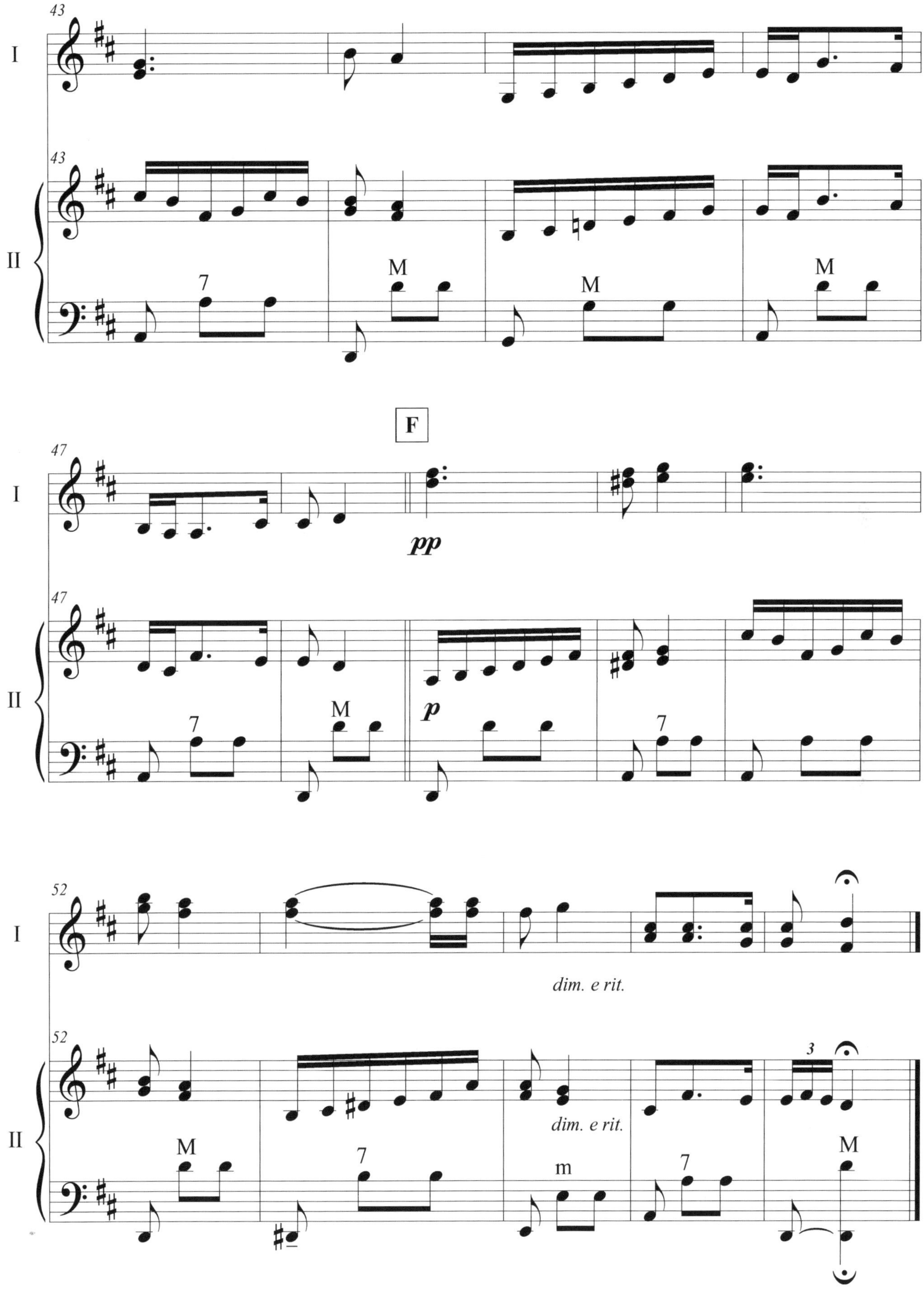
43
I
II
7
M
47
F
pp
p
52
dim. e rit.
m
3

Mi Posso Maritar

Sicilian
Arr. by Carole Gatwood

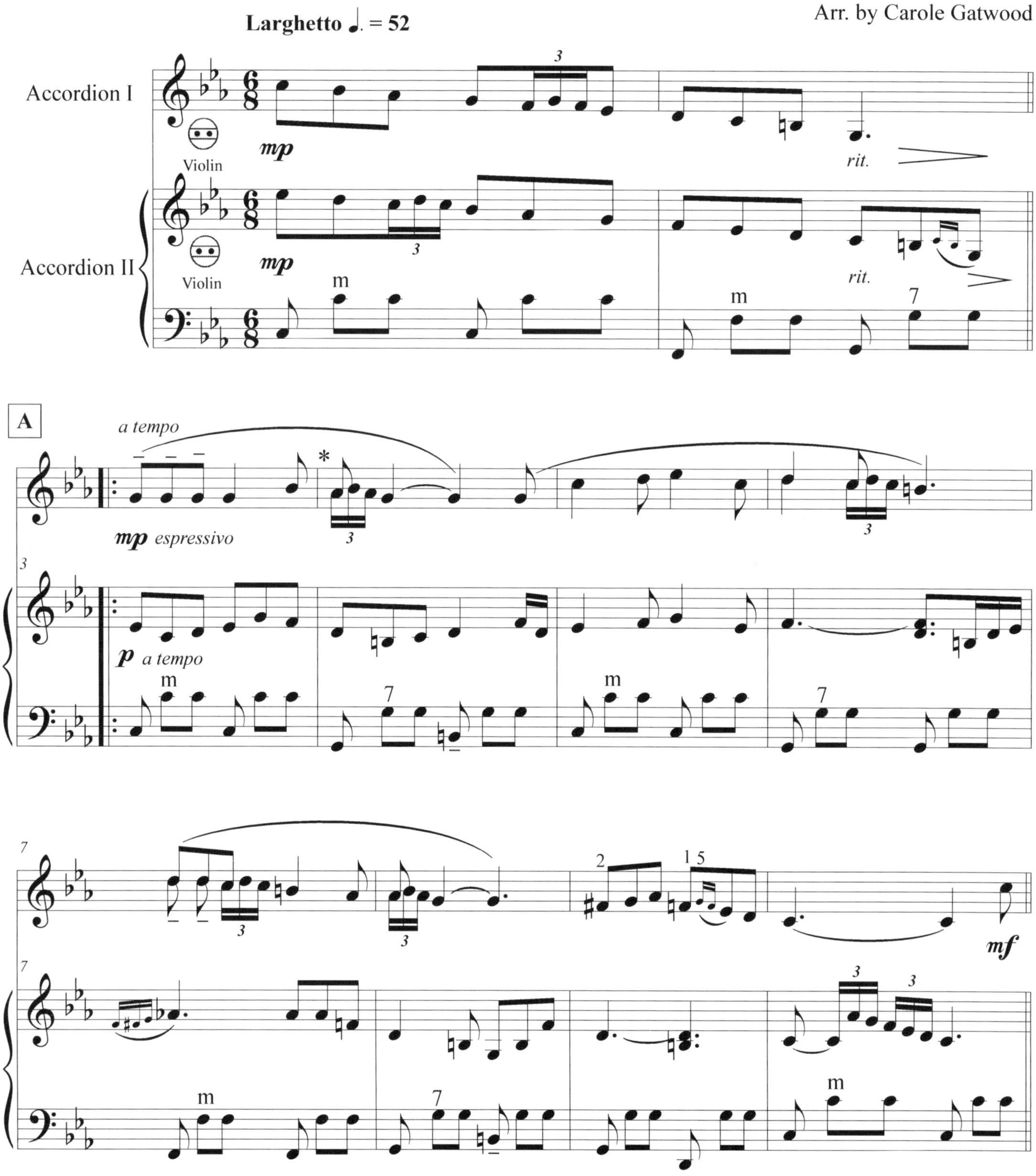

* Split stems offer a choice of playing the melody simply the first time and more embellished on the repeat.

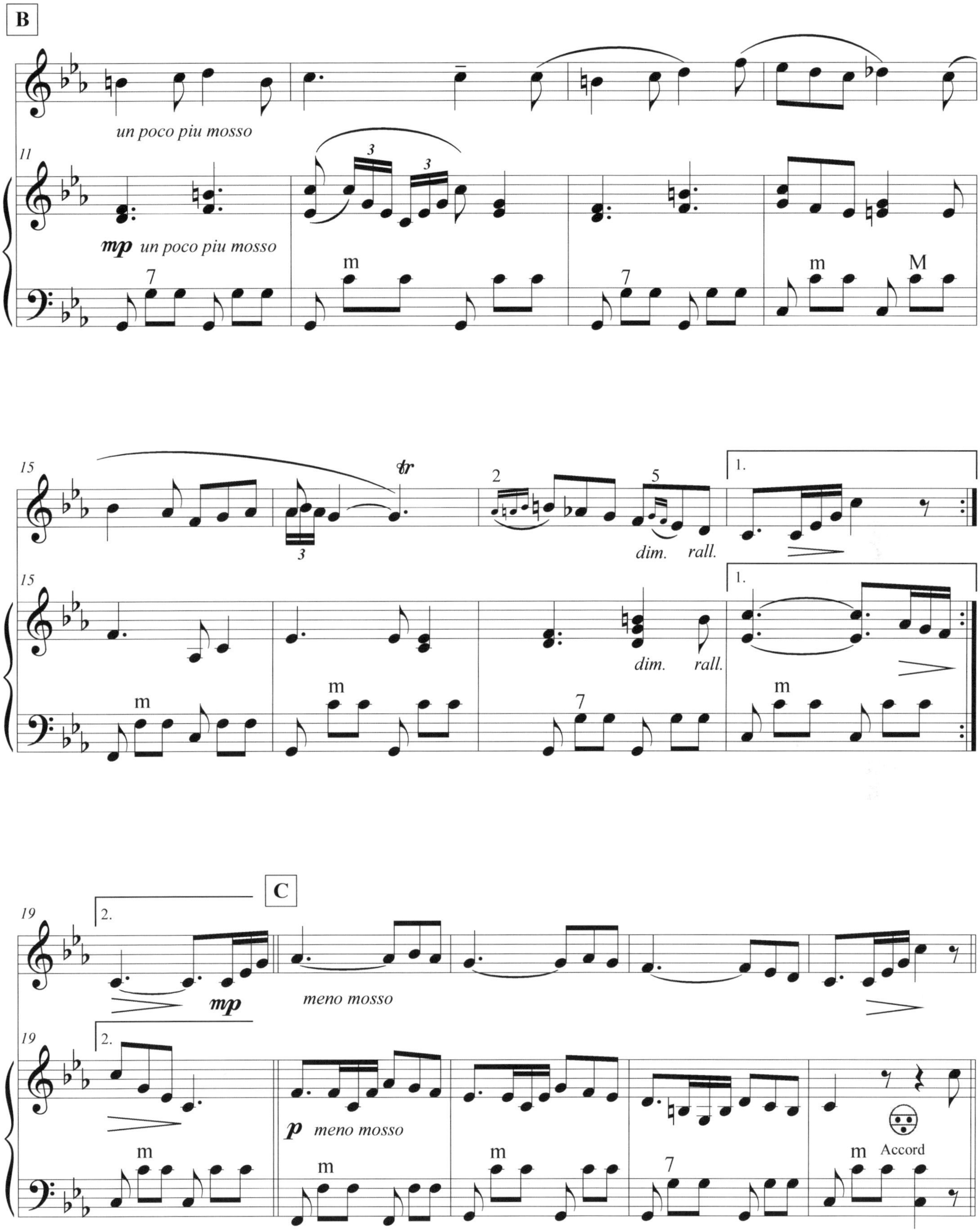
B
I
II
un poco piu mosso
mp un poco piu mosso
dim.
rall.
C
meno mosso
p meno mosso
Accord

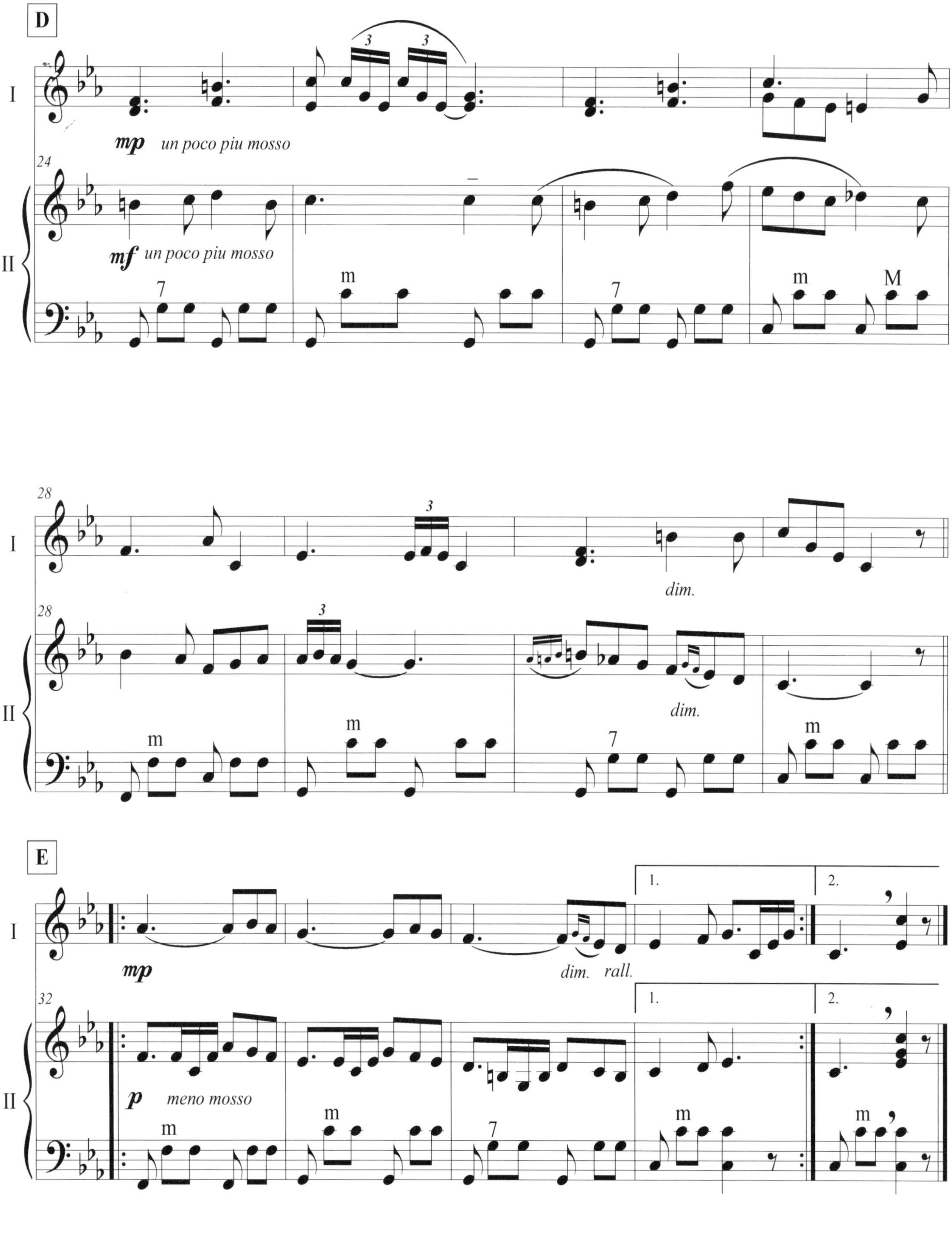
D
I
II
mp un poco piu mosso
24
mf un poco piu mosso
28
dim.
E
1.
2.
mp
dim. rall.
32
p meno mosso

I Primi Amori

Canzone di Carditello, "My First Loves"

Guglielmo Cottrau
Arr. by Carole Gatwood

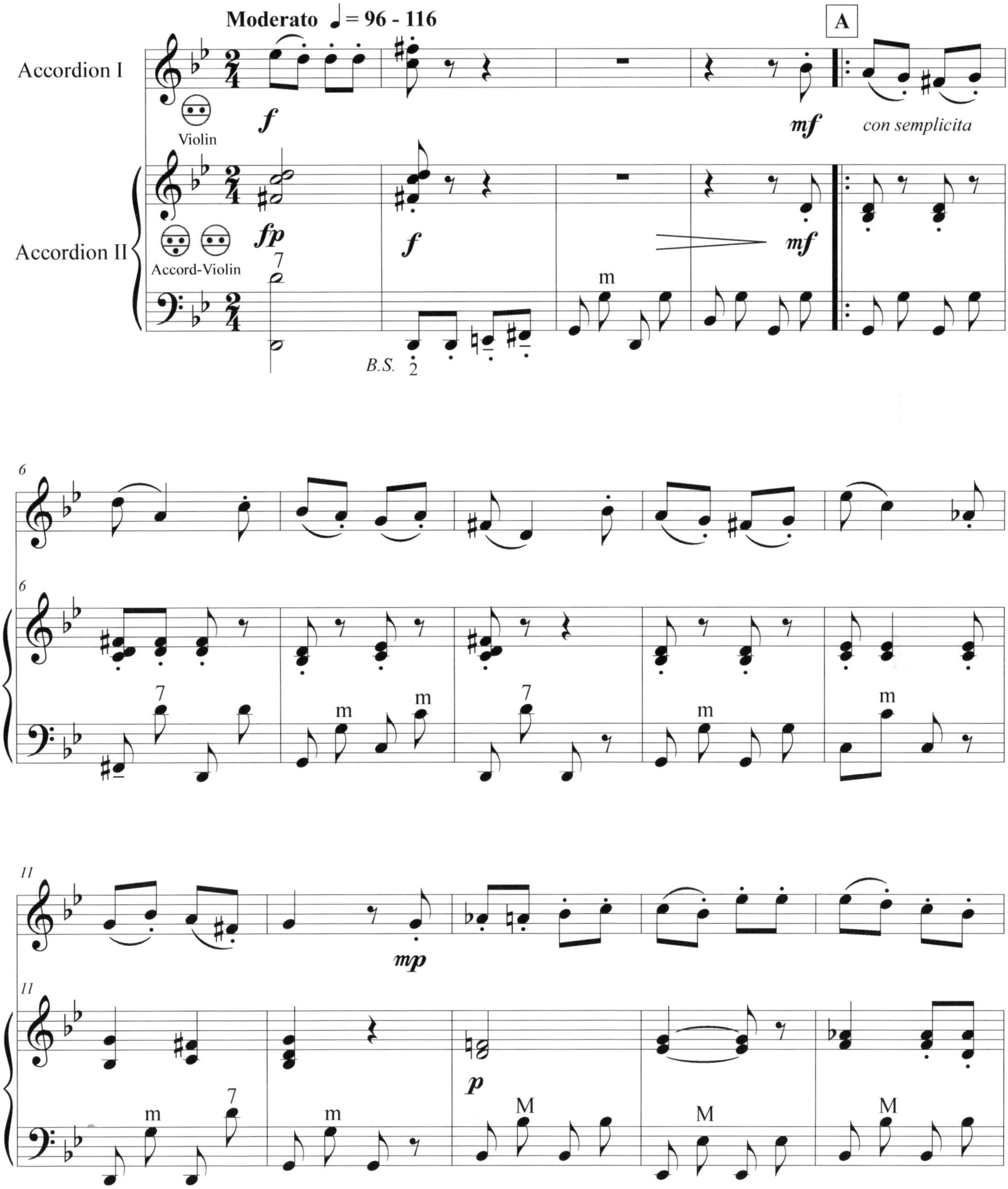

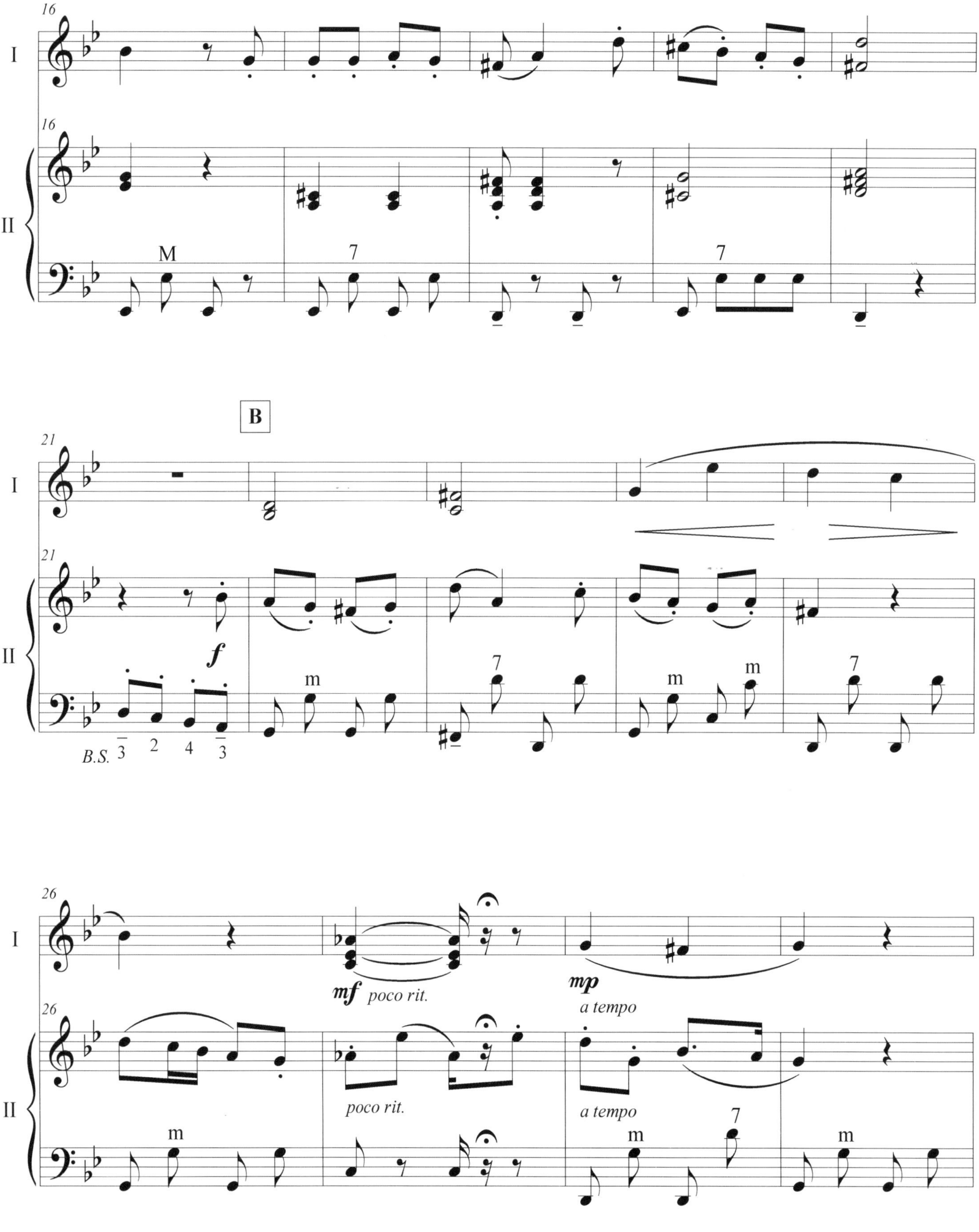
I
II
B
B.S.
poco rit.
a tempo
poco rit.
a tempo

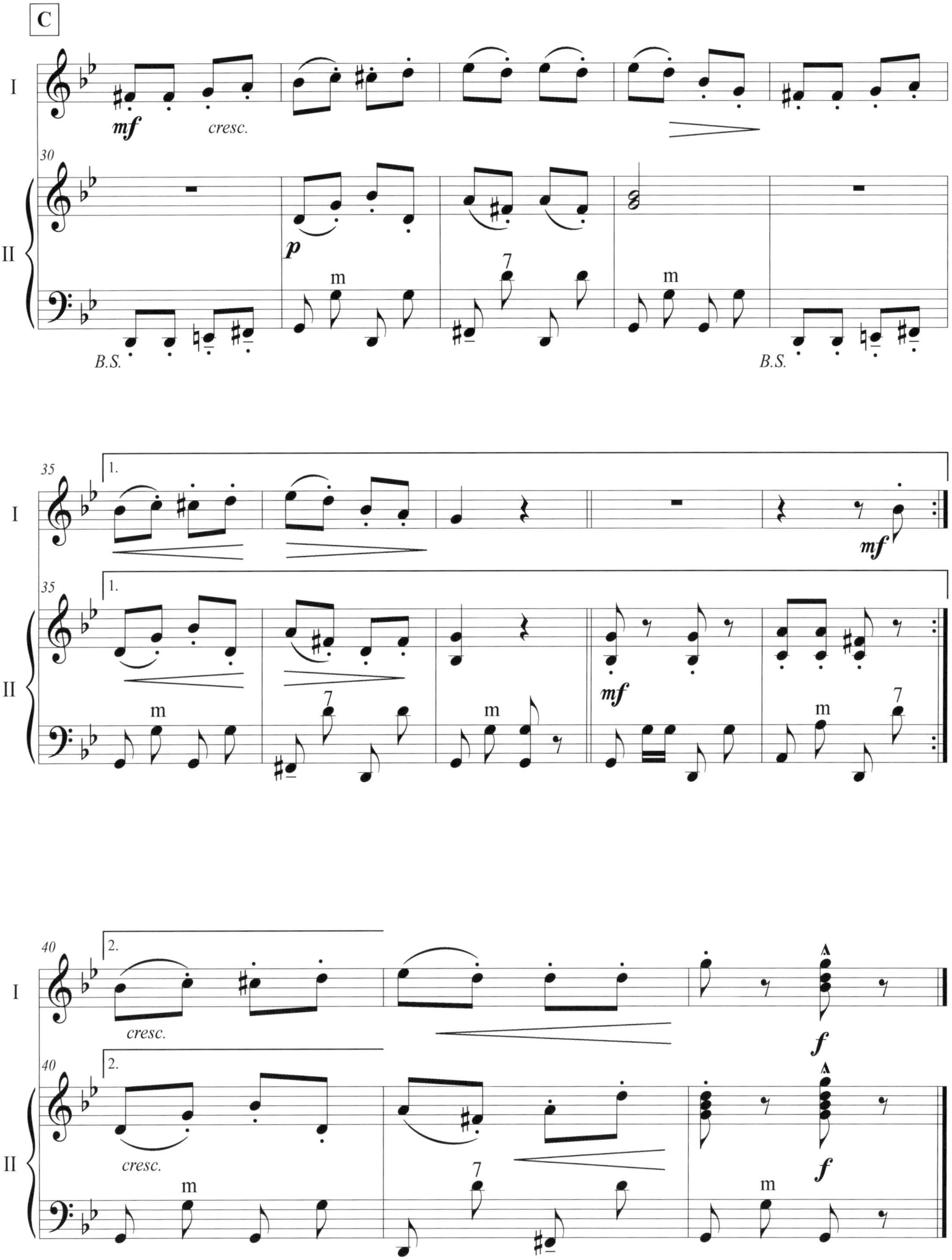
C
I
II
30
mf
cresc.
p
m
7
B.S.
35
1.
40
2.
f

Mi Lasciasti in Abbandono

"You Abandoned Me"

Arr. by Carole Gatwood

Agitato (♪ = 144 - 168)

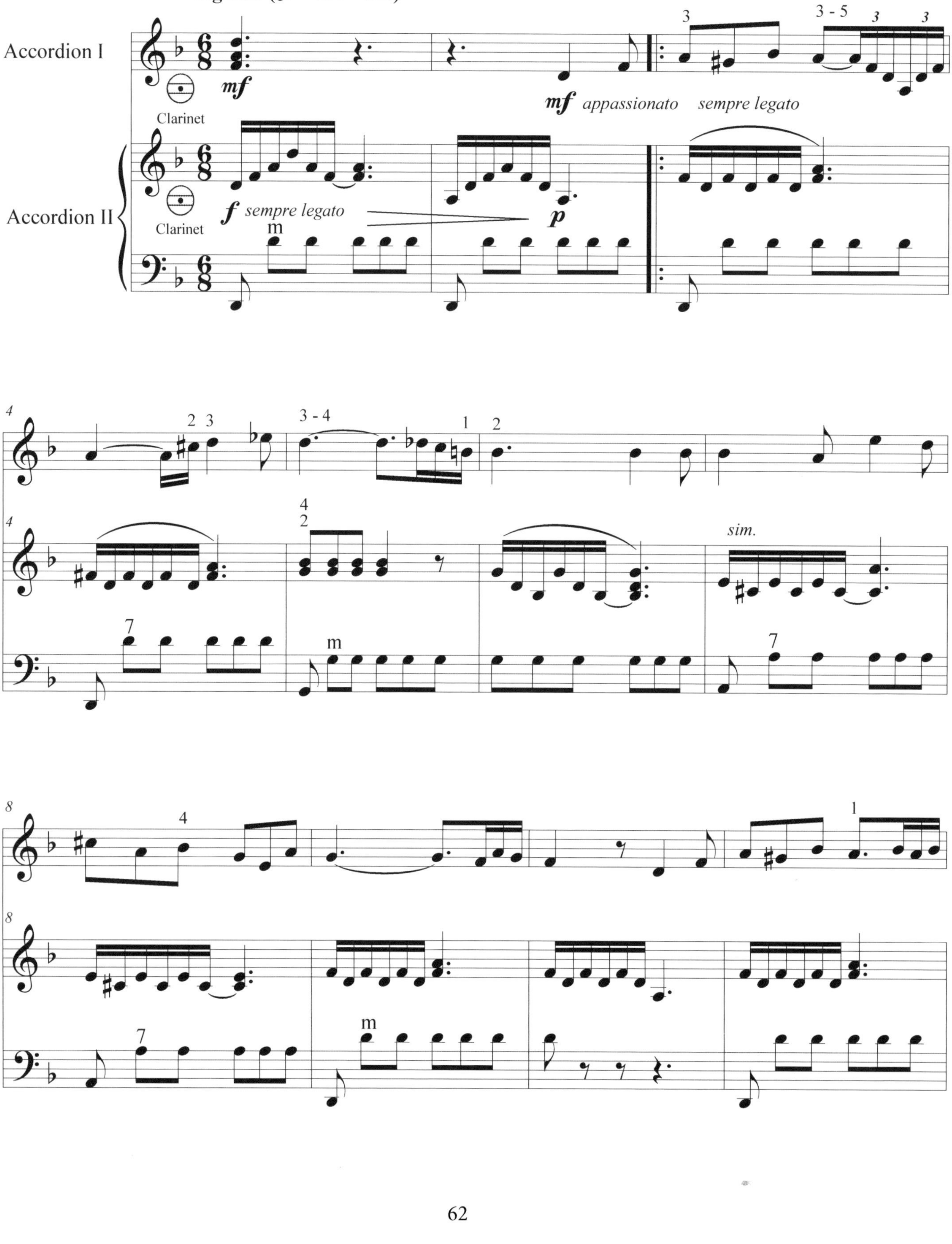

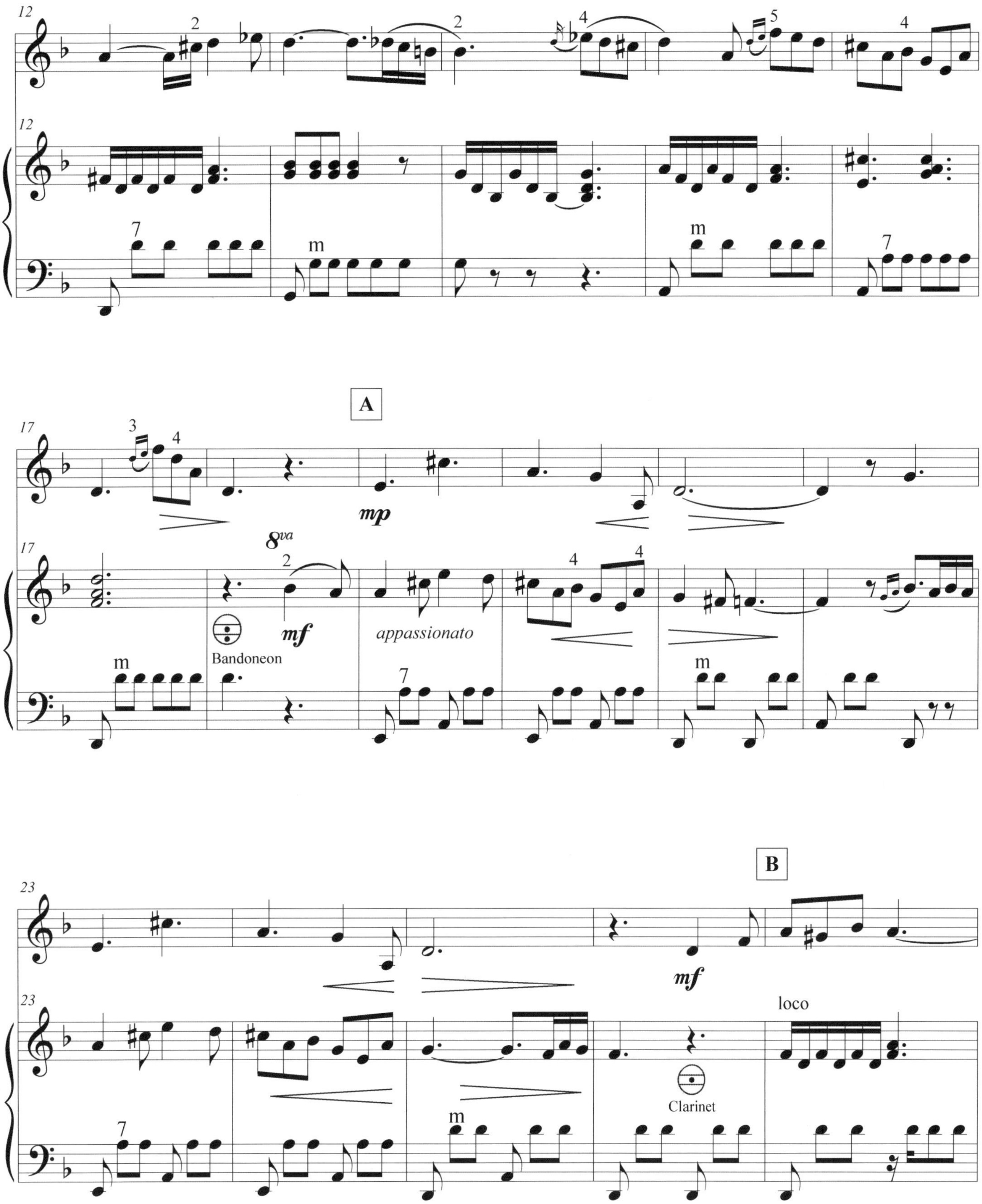
I
II
A
mp
8va
mf
Bandoneon
appassionato
B
loco
Clarinet

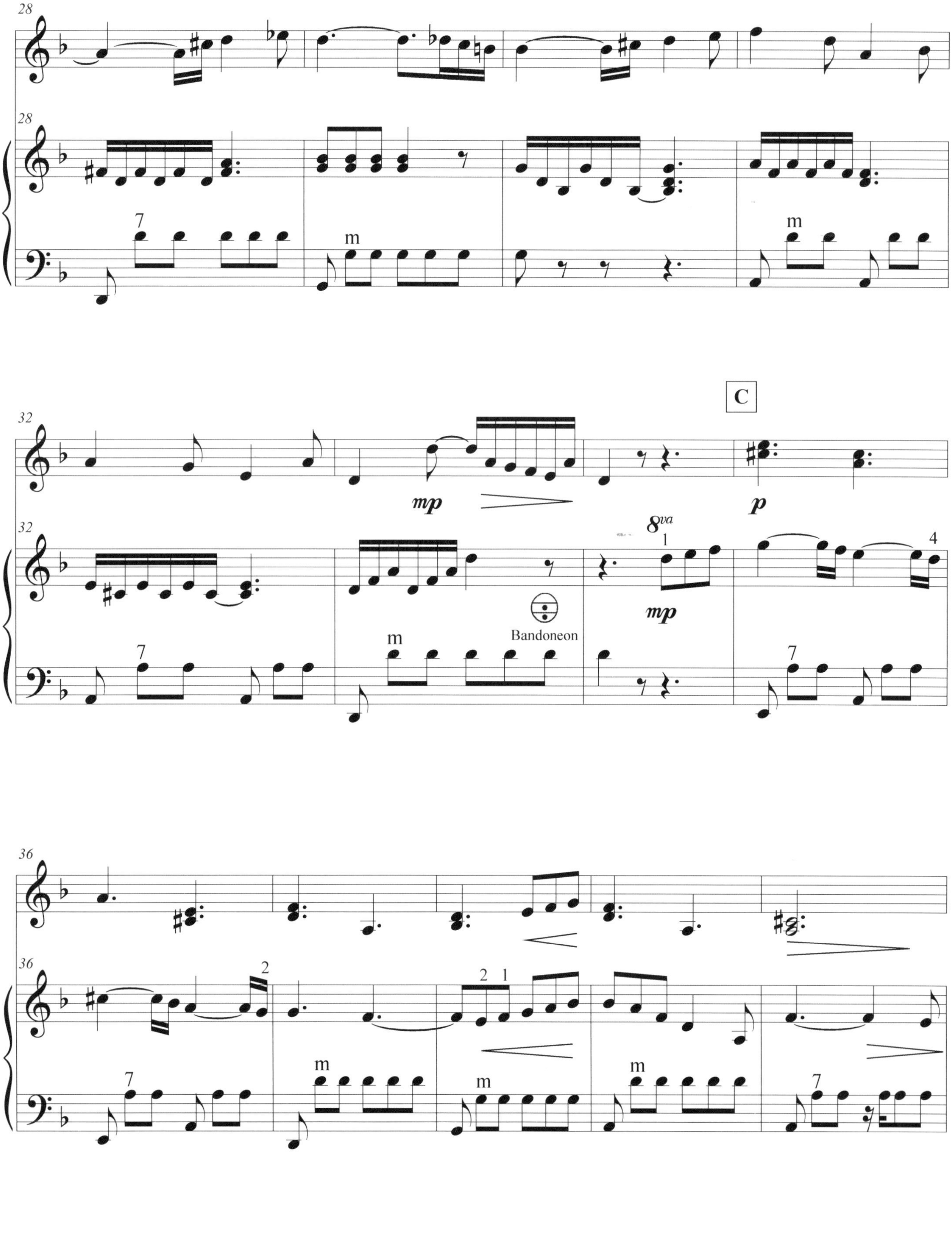
28
I
II
32
C
mp
p
8va
Bandoneon
36

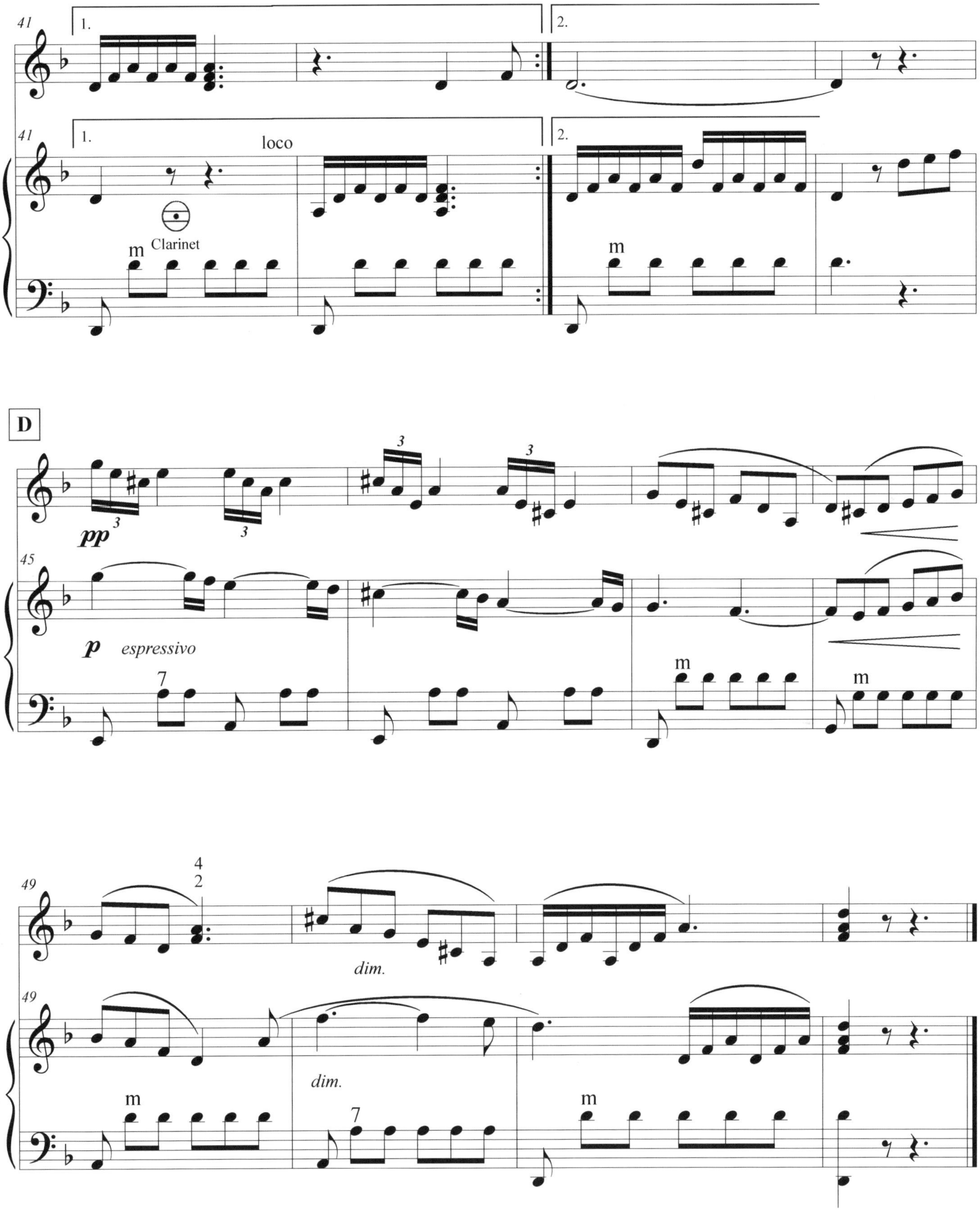
41
1.
2.
I
II
loco
Clarinet
m
D
pp
45
p espressivo
7
49
4
2
dim.

Forturella

Canzone Napoletana

Guglielmo Cottrau
Arr. by Carole Gatwood

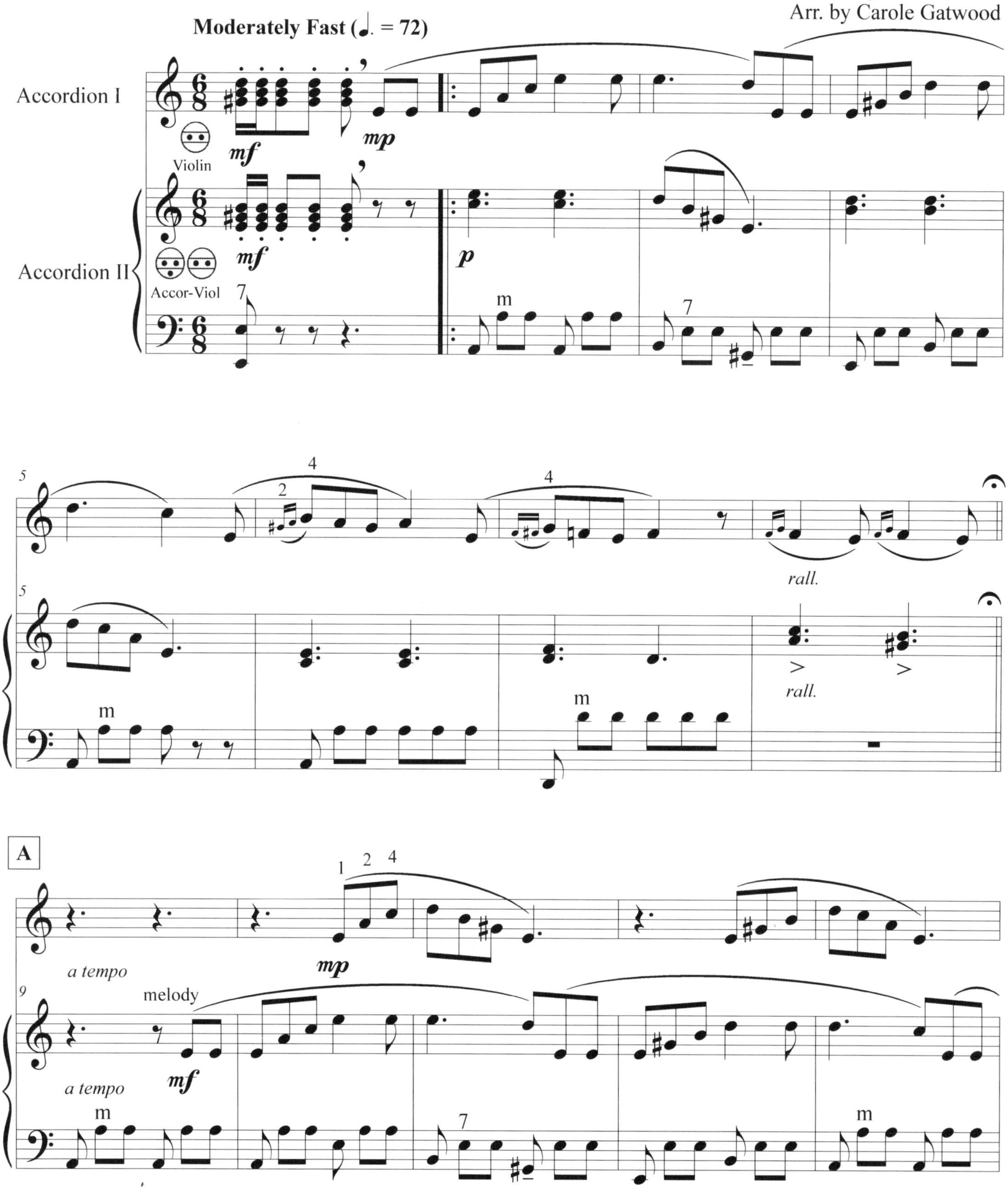

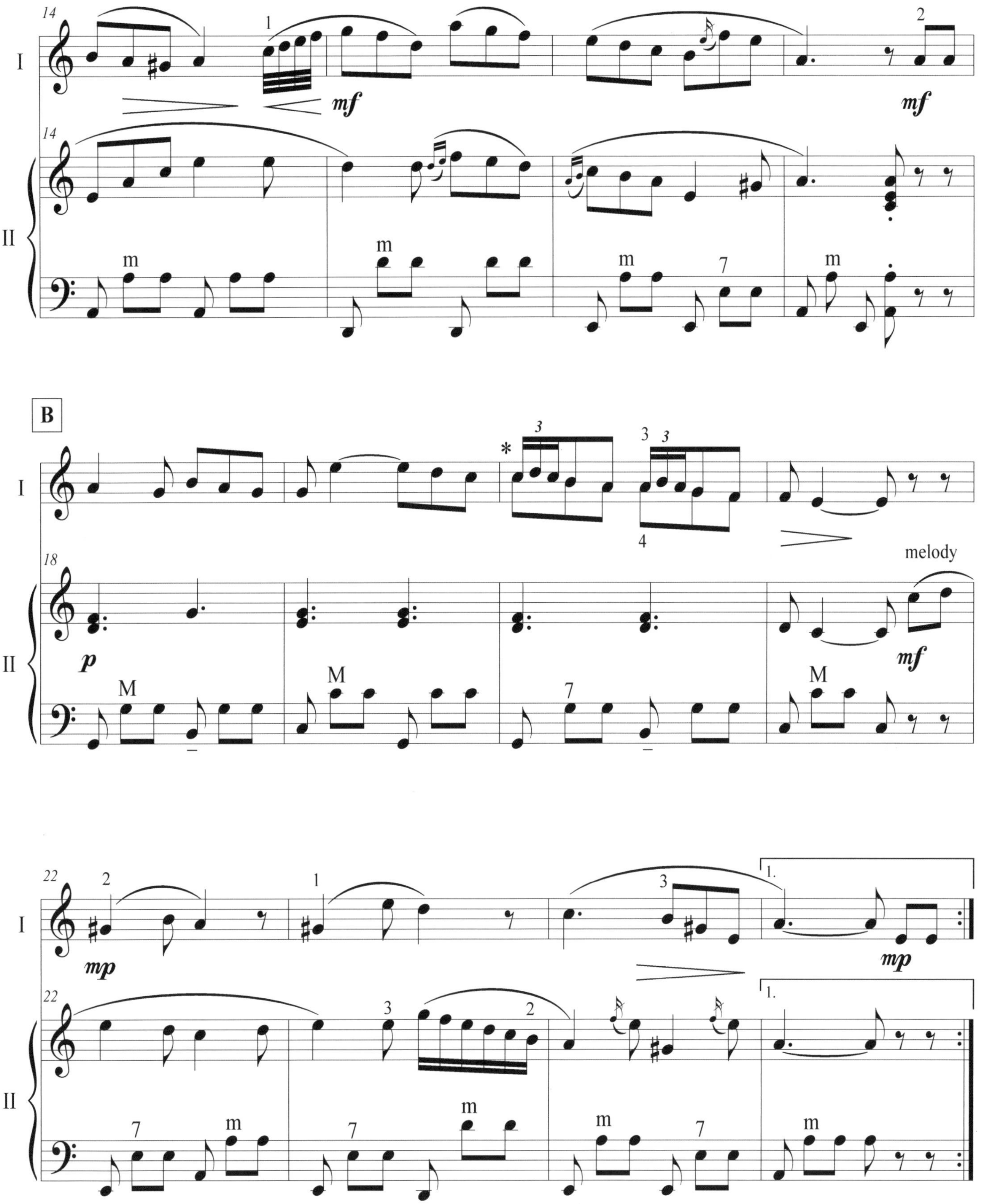

* Split stems in measure 20 give the option of playing straight eighth notes the first time and triplets on the repeat, if desired.

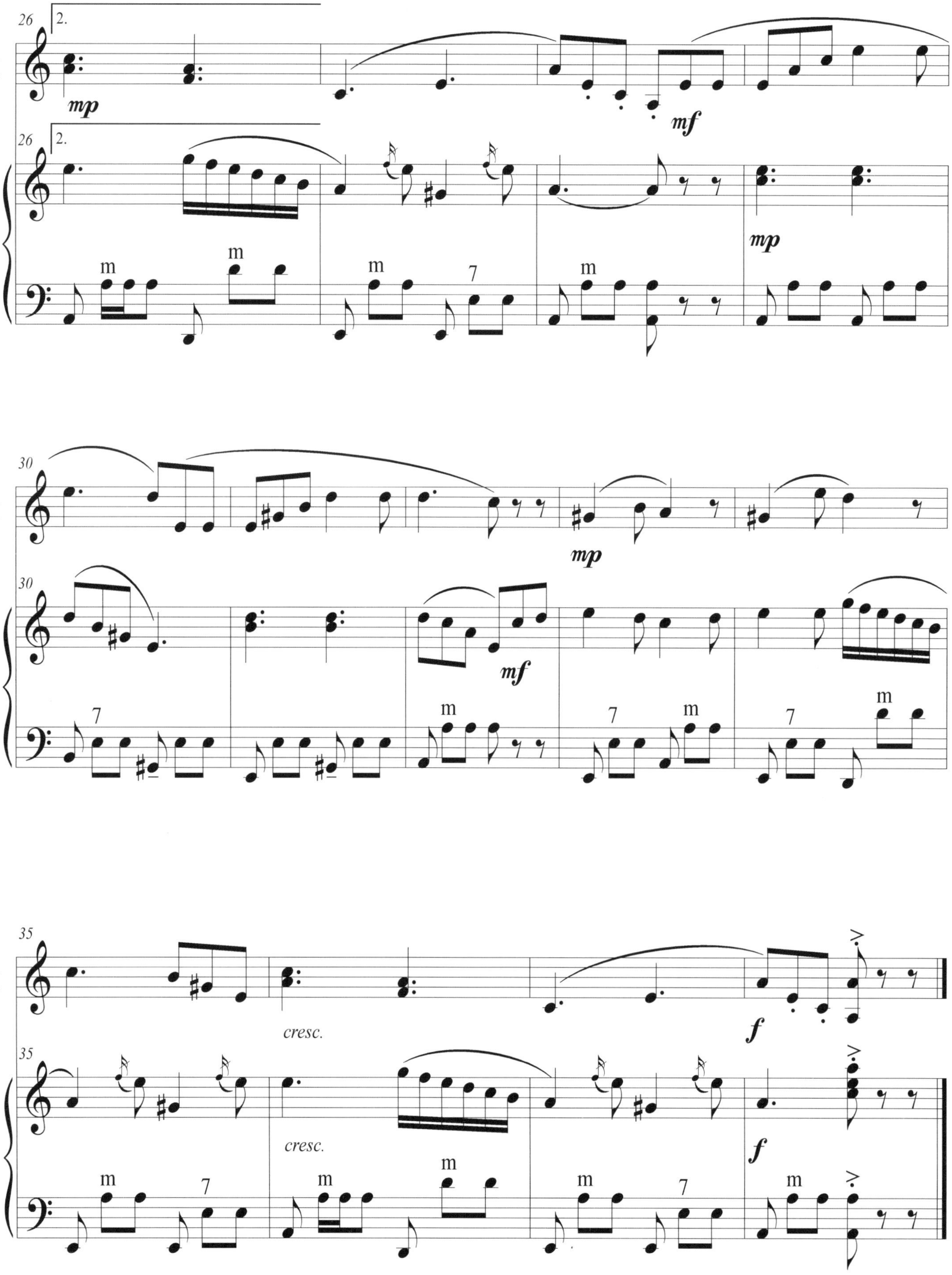
26
2.
I
II
mp
mf
m
7
30
35
cresc.
f